AGNES I. NUMER - SERMONS

VOLUME 6 - ISAIAH 58 - TIME TO RUN

AGNES I. NUMER

Agnes I. Numer – Time to Run
Sermons - Volume 6

© 2021 All Nations International

ISBN: 978-1-955759-04-5

Unless otherwise indicated, all Scripture quotations are taken from the Holy Bible, King James Version - Public Domain

Compiled by All Nations International

Messages transcribed by: Jennene Jeffrey

Editors: Virginia Russell, Annella Whitehead, Kathy Vanzandt

Chief editor: Nona Babich

Published by: Teresa Skinner Publishing

Photos in this book are of peoples lives who have been touched through Rev. Agnes I. Numer

DEDICATION

To the Giant Takers

GIANT-TAKERS

"The generation that now sits at your feet."

— C. Johnson

CONTENTS

Foreword	ix
Preface	xi
Thy Word Is a Lamp	1
Isaiah 58 - Time to Run	14
Transfiguration	32
Under New Management	42
Waiting Upon the Lord	52
We All Have a Choice	63
What Does He Require of Us?	78
The Vision No Longer Tarries	91
Allowing God's Perfect Peace	102
The Plumbline	123
Lord, You Have Ordained Peace for Us	135
Faith Worketh By Love	141
Come Up Higher in His Love	156
Pass It On	169
Prophecy through Kim Clement	176
Photos	178
About the Author	179
More Sermons by Agnes I. Numer	181

FOREWORD

If God would miraculously use a tiny, little, 2 ½ pound baby, born in 1915 …who never saw an incubator. And, grant her long life, so that He would show His Love, to others through her… Then just maybe, this God could mend our broken hearts and put His love there, and use us?

When we see a life like this…We are faced with a decision:

To Continue Life as Usual.

Or RISE to the unusual.

Thus, was the life of Rev. Agnes I Numer.

May these sermons challenge your life as they have ours.

TERESA SKINNER
EXECUTIVE DIRECTOR
ALL NATIONS INTERNATIONAL

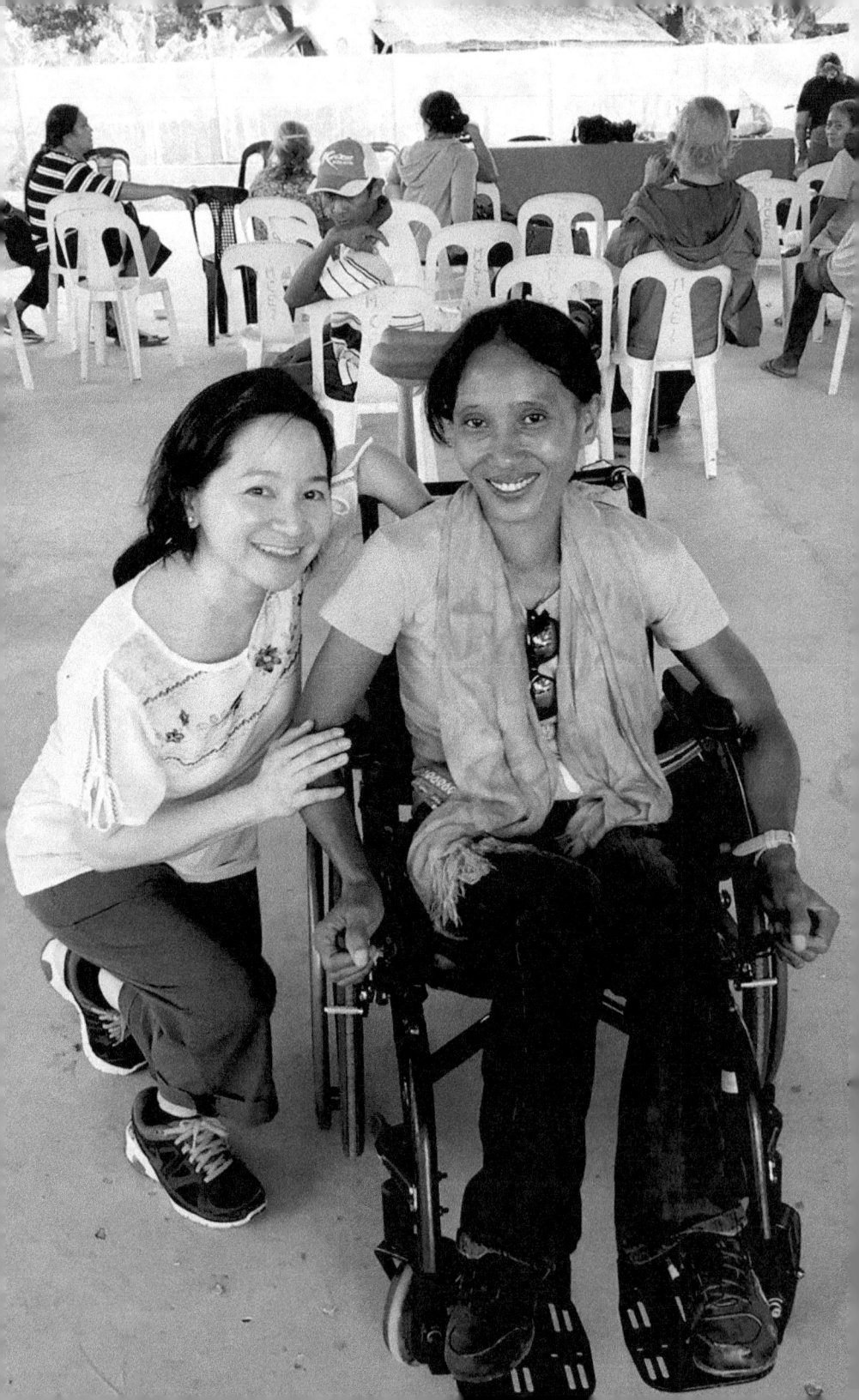

PREFACE

If you ever wanted to see the Holy Spirit, all you had to do was gaze into Agnes' eyes.

If you ever wanted to hear the Holy Spirit, all you had to do was ask Agnes to tell a story.

If you ever wanted to know what love is, all you had to do was ask Agnes for a hug....

Anonymous
Friend

Facing photo: Dr. Lilibeth Say - founder, Wheel Chair Harvest Project - Philippines (2021)

FEED THE HUNGRY

LET THE OPPRESSED GO FREE

DEMONSTRATE
THE LOVE OF GOD

UNDO THE HEAVY BURDENS

CLOTHE THE NAKED

THY WORD IS A LAMP

The 176 verses of Psalm 119 are all God's precepts.

> Thy testimonies have I taken as an heritage for ever: for they *are* the rejoicing of my heart. Psalm 119:111

> Thy word *is* a lamp unto my feet, and a light unto my path. Psalm 119:105

I believe there are 176 verses in Psalm 119. Do you want to memorize it? The reason I'm saying this is that all 176 verses are His precepts.

> Psalm 119:11 Thy word have I hid in mine heart, that I might not sin against thee. 12 Blessed *art* thou, O LORD: teach me thy statutes. 13 With my lips have I declared all the judgments of thy mouth. 14 I have rejoiced in the way of thy testimonies, as *much as* in all riches. 15 I will meditate in thy precepts, and have respect unto thy ways. 16 I will delight

myself in thy statutes: I will not forget thy word. Psalm 119:11-16

Ps. 119:9 Wherewithal shall a young man cleanse his way? by taking heed *thereto* according to thy word. 10 With my whole heart have I sought thee: O let me not wander from thy commandments. Psalm 119:9-10

As we are studying all of this that is happening today, concerning that scripture, which God spoke in Isaiah 28 remember that precept is a commandment or direction given as a rule of action or conduct. His word says,

Thy word have I hid in mine heart, that I might not sin against thee. Psalm 119:11

Isaiah 28:10 says,

For precept must be upon precept, precept upon precept; line upon line, line upon line; here a little, and there a little. Isaiah 28:10

We're talking about spiritual things; God is teaching us to hear Him with our ears. How do you think you're going to follow Him if you don't know His voice?

Blessed are the undefiled in the way, who walk in the law of the Lord. Psalm 119:1

How do we know His law? He's given us precept upon precept, this is His law and He has given it a little here and a little there, line upon line. If we didn't hear it the first time we can still receive it for its precept upon precept; line must be upon line; here a little and there a little. He's speaking to us in a very special way because He's teaching us to hear His voice, to believe in Him and to know Him.

How are you going to know the Lord? You have to know His voice! You have to know His voice or you don't know Him. You can say, "I'm a Christian, I'm born again, and I know Jesus;" but how much do you know Him? We have to get acquainted with Him. How much does somebody know you if they just say hello to you? I know a lot of people say they know me. They may know me by name, but really, I don't know them. The Lord is bringing us into an intimate relationship with Him for He said that He's closer than a Father, closer than a Mother, a Brother or a Sister.

Where is He? Where does He live? You say, "He lives in our hearts!" How is He going to live in our hearts if we don't know anything about Him? We need to praise Him, prayer is another way, and by worshiping Him. That's what draws us near to Him so we can know Him as He says, "I give you my rest." How many of you get weary and you long for rest and you don't get any? He said, "Come unto me and I will give you rest; come and you will find rest for your souls."

Now why don't we come to Him? Sometimes we don't hear His voice; sometimes when He says, "Come and walk with me, or come and pray to me," what do we do? We say, "We'll go out and play ball first or something else first." The Lord says, "I'm calling you away now to come to me and hear my voice."

See what He's saying. He says, "I will sing to you." Did you know the Lord wants to sing to us? He can't sing to us if we don't know His voice. If we don't know His voice He could be screaming at us. We would know if we would get quiet before Him and say, "Lord, I want to know you." Just because our sins are forgiven doesn't mean we know Him. How much do we know Him? This 119th Psalm brings us in, so tremendously, to know Him and to know His word; all 176 verses.

Oh, how wonderful is our God. He said in Matthew,

> Come unto me, all ye that labor and are heavy laden, and I will give you rest. Matthew 11:28

He cried out to the children of Israel; He brought them out of the bondage of Egypt. He said to Moses, "I want to be your God and I want you to be my people." High up in the mountain, He reveals Himself to Moses. The people said, "We don't want You Lord; we'll take Moses but we don't want you." Mind you, He had just brought them out of captivity in the land of Egypt, where they were slaves; where they were beaten and treated very cruelly.

God, through Moses, leads them out of Egypt, across the Red Sea, and takes care of them. He opens that sea so they can walk out on dry land, back into His Promised Land. What did they do, very quickly, when they got to the Promised Land? Moses has disappeared they don't know where he is. He's high up in the mountain talking to God. God is telling him, "I have some written commandments for you." Do you know who wrote those commandments? God Himself with His finger! He wrote every one of those commandments He wants us to keep.

What happened while He was up there and God was writing the beautiful wonderful commandments? Down there in the valley, they were so hungry to go back into bondage and be treated like slaves, that they made a golden image and worshiped it. People are still worshipping other gods everywhere in the world. The Christians are doing it, too. If God is not first in our lives, if we're not drawing close to Him, if we haven't hidden His word in our hearts, then we're in trouble.

What happened when Moses came down off of the mountain? They had taken everything God had let them bring out of Egypt and offered it to idols! All that God had given them was destroyed. God wrote the law with His own finger because of the love He had for these people He had created. When Moses came down, what happens to the tablets? Why were they broken? The people had already broken the laws in their hearts!

"Oh, God, save us from this horrible condition in Egypt." They were slaves and were treated very badly and had to make the bricks without straw. Here they were crying, "Take us out of this." But when God brought them out they forgot Him. God spoke to Moses in His anger and said, "I'll just blot them all out." Moses said, "Then who is going to honor your name and your word if you blot them all out?" Moses pleaded, "Forgive them; if you won't, blot my name out, too."

It was Moses that was obeying the Lord; the rest of them weren't. Here are these beautiful commandments written by the finger of God and here was a people called by His name and they were worshiping a golden calf of their own making. They didn't know Him and weren't grateful that they were brought out. They said, "Let us go back into Egypt, back into slavery."

God takes us when we're born again and forgives all our sins. Then what happens? Our flesh says, "I want a cigarette or a drink of beer or whiskey or drugs." If we listen to our flesh rather than the Lord, the devil will keep us bound by these things. We don't let go of them and because we don't, the devil still holds onto us. We need to say to the devil, "I don't want this, you keep it." If we're willing God will take these desires instantly and sweep us clean of everything.

God is saying to us, "I give you a commandment that you love the Lord thy God with all thy heart, with all thy soul and with all thy might." Does that leave any room for anything else? Jesus is saying, "Come unto me all ye that labor and are heavy laden and I will give you rest and you can cause the weary to rest; but we fight back. We're no match for our flesh or the devil; because the devil is going to rule our flesh when we yield to these things. God is saying, "Come unto me and I will give you rest. I will take all of this out of you and give you my rest and my peace." But we fight with Him, we argue about our precious flesh that's only destruction. We will never win with our flesh; it has to die.

The Lord said, "Precept upon precept, here a little, there a little, and line upon line." I've taught this scripture for so long that people thought I didn't know another. I did it because the Holy Ghost wanted it to penetrate. The Lord said to me that just because they have ears, it doesn't mean they hear.

God has given us His word that we might walk in His way. Before Jesus came it wasn't possible for us to be forgiven without the shedding of the blood of animals. After Jesus came and shed His blood on that cross it is possible, through His grace, for us to keep the commandments. It is through His word and His righteous blood that we no longer have to kill animals. His precious blood was shed for the forgiveness of our sins. God will take away our stony hearts and give us a clean heart of flesh and put a new spirit within us. We will then have His peace, His love, His joy and His righteousness.

He's talking about these children of Israel as they came out of Egypt. He had for them a new heart and was going to take out the stony heart and put in a heart of flesh and He had a new spirit to place within them, but they did want Him.

When God does this for us there is no reason for us to sin. We're not connected with the old Adam any more. We're set free from him because we become a new creature in a new creation with a new heart, and He gives us His Spirit that enables us to keep His commandments and statutes. If we don't get close to Him and allow Him to speak to us we soon wonder off in the direction of our flesh. He has given us a new heart, a new mind and a new soul and set us free with His precious spirit to guide us. But we have to hear it and follow it or else our flesh and the devil will come and disrupt God's plan for us.

Moses was in God's presence on the mountain. It's so awesome to imagine God writing these commandments with His own finger. Moses was there watching Him down below in the valley. Aaron was helping to build the calf, Moses' right hand man. Not anybody but Moses was standing with God; how sad God must have been. "Moses, just blot them all out! They don't deserve my love or to have come out of Egypt or to come to know me."

God said, I'll give you a new heart. I'll take out your stony heart and give you a pure heart and new spirit and place my Spirit within you. But here they were down there worshiping, very loudly, the golden calf. So loud was their noise that it came up the mountain where God was giving Moses the 10 commandments.

> And thou shalt love the LORD thy God with all thine heart, and with all thy soul, and with all thy might. Deuteronomy 6:5

He said, "Come unto me, I'll not cast you out. I'll take your sins and throw them away and destroy them and I will lead you by my word and my Spirit. And I will bring you unto myself."

How many obey and tell the truth? They cover their lies because they don't want anybody to know it's a lie. I'm going to tell you one thing I know, God is coming to Sommer Haven by the mighty power of His Spirit. I don't think persons will continue to get by with cheating, stealing or lying here; because God has come to bring this Word of Life to us boldly. I'm praying that the Holy Spirit will come and there will not be one thing that anybody will get by with. The scripture says to bring every thought into captivity. This is what God wants of us. He wants every thought to be brought into captivity so that Jesus might be the only one in our lives, nothing else. Not our flesh or the devil, but Jesus.

He's calling us unto Himself and this word is a light unto our feet and a lamp unto our path. God said to have a Christian school. There are other children that don't go to a Christian school and they don't hear about Jesus every day in a class room. They don't have the privilege of playing or singing anywhere they want to sing and worship, but we have that privilege.

Let me tell you the results of Isaiah 58. People decided they would make lies their refuge and false hood their covering. Then God said, "I'm going to send a deluge and storms and everything." They laughed at Him. They said we're hid under lies. We're covered with false hood and you aren't going to effect us when that storm comes. Do you know when the storm is coming? It's come right now over the whole earth; because man said we've made lies our refuge and false hood our covering.

I lay in Zion for a foundation a stone, a precious corner stone, a sure foundation, and no man is going to hide from it. They'll be destroyed by it if they don't receive it. God is saying that He has laid before us a sure foundation, Jesus Christ in us. But with Him come His laws, His rules and way of life; His way of direction and action and conduct. He is saying, "Put it in your heart."

They said, "We are not going to do it because we going to do our own thing and our things are not going to affect us." But today through every part of the world God is sending storms and floods; He's sweeping the whole earth. In Orcia, India alone, 27,000 villages were swept away. Why were they swept away? It's God's storm and God's judgment. They said no to God and they burned the missionaries. "We don't want God or His anointed;" so He sends a cyclone and destroys 27,000 villages. "We're not afraid of Him. We don't want to keep His Word; we can lie, cheat and steal and live as we want."

You better not because God is moving in His judgment upon the whole earth. That which He spoke about in Isaiah 28 is now sweeping the whole wide world. That's how it is right now, things are happening all over the world and judgment and justice are covering the earth. If we can be in with what God is doing, He will use us. We can't play around with the flesh and the devil or we will be swept away by the storm. He has given us His word and it is true and He is faithful. What we need to do is not lie to God or play games with Him. We have to hear what He's saying. We have to do it God's way.

They say, "We're covered with lies and false hoods and your avalanche of storms is not going to affect us." God sent a storm that took out 27,000 villages. Don't say God can't do it. Turn your lives over to Him and He will take out those things and fill you with His love and His word and then the enemy won't be able to lie to you or trick you; because you will know God's voice and the enemy's voice. You will not follow Satan but you will follow the voice of the Lord as He guides you by His Word and His Spirit.

God is calling us unto Himself so He can love us and we can rest in that love. If we argue with Him and want our way, we will lose. It's Gods way that's coming forth and in Him we're going to move and live and have our being. He's calling us unto Himself, into that which He chose for the children of Israel and they refused. He's still calling us to come and receive it. The children of Israel didn't know the Lord, but they had His commandments. They knew the Living God, but they refused to serve Him.

We have to be careful that we're not holding onto anything, but to realize that the Lord has given us His commandments. He has given us His Word and His Word will stand forever. The earth will pass away, but His word will never pass away. The word He has given to us, He wants to hide it in our hearts that we might not sin against Him. We must realize that everything else is going to pass away but His kingdom will be forever. His love, provision and His glory will be forever. We have to walk the way He has called us to walk, according to His laws and according to the statutes which His Spirit gives to us to guide us so that we do not go in the path of the enemy or the way of our own flesh.

Just cry out to Him and ask that He take away everything and give you a new heart, with His love and His Spirit that we might keep His statutes and His laws. God has placed it before us; but we need to realize that God requires us to do exactly what He calls us to do. It is not impossible; it's only impossible if we refuse to do it. That's our fault, it's not God's.

> Psalm 119:90 Thy faithfulness *is* unto all generations: thou hast established the earth, and it abideth. 91 They continue this day according to thine ordinances: for all *are* thy servants. 92 Unless thy law *had been* my delights, I should then have perished in mine affliction. 93 I will never forget thy precepts: for with them thou hast quickened me. 94 I *am* thine, save me; for I have sought thy precepts. 95 The wicked have waited for me to destroy me: *but* I will consider thy testimonies. 96 I have seen an end of all perfection: *but* thy commandment is exceeding broad. — MEM — 97 O how love I thy law! it *is* my meditation all the day. 98 Thou through thy commandments hast made me wiser than mine enemies: for they *are* ever with me. 99 I have more understanding than all my teachers: for thy testimonies *are* my meditation. 100 I understand more than the ancients, because I keep thy precepts. 101. I have refrained my feet from every evil way, that I might keep thy word. 102 I have not departed from thy judgments: for thou hast taught me. 103 How sweet are thy words unto my taste! *yea, sweeter*

than honey to my mouth! 104 Through thy precepts I get understanding: therefore I hate every false way. Psalm 119:90-104

Why was God so upset in Isaiah 28? Because here are His precepts and laws! The drunkards of Ephraim said, "We'll stay under lies and false hoods, they are our covering." But the Lord said

> Behold, the Lord hath a mighty and strong one, which as a tempest of hail and a destroying storm, as a flood of mighty waters overflowing, shall cast down to the earth with the hand. Isaiah 28:2

This is the penalty today. This same word goes out to the nations and to every individual. We're doing the same thing they were doing in their day. God is calling for a reckoning day, according to His word. I long to see the Holy Ghost come in this place so strong that people will fall on their faces before God.

I was in college and the Spirit of the Lord was calling. It wasn't a Pentecostal group, just people who loved the Lord. The Spirit of the Lord came with such might and one of the girls was rejecting him. We started up the stairs and she was rejecting the Spirit of the Lord. And as she came up to her room Satan met her at the door. She screamed when she saw him. I ran up the steps and she said, "Satan was standing at my door." She fell on her face and began to ask the Lord to forgive her. She met Satan face to face and I will never forget that night. We rushed up there to pray with her and she gave her life to the Lord. She couldn't resist Him any longer. She found out where she was headed, right into the arms of Satan, to be forever destroyed.

The Lord has forgiven us. The Word says,

> Thy word *is* a lamp unto my feet and a light unto my path. I have sworn and I will perform *it* and will keep thy righteous judgments. Psalm 119:105

Father, I thank you for this word. Quicken it to each one of our hearts that we might know and obey you. Amen.

Agnes I Numer with long time friend and coworker Linda Beard

ISAIAH 58 - TIME TO RUN

Father, we thank You. We praise You, Lord Jesus, that You've given unto us Your light that we might live. Lord Jesus, we praise You, we thank You. You not only died for us, but You gave us a way of life that even in this world we might know how to walk with You, to keep Your Word and obey You. Lord Jesus, we ask You to make this Word real to us as You have given it to us. We ask you to renew the vision before us, Oh God, for Your glory. And in Your name, Jesus, we ask it, Amen.

His Call by His Word

Many years ago, the Lord gave me a scripture. He gave it to me when I was a teenager:

> "I will stand upon my watch, and set me upon the tower, and will watch to see what He will say unto me, and what I shall answer when I am reproved. And the LORD answered me, and said, write the vision, and make it plain upon tables,

that he may run that readeth it. For the vision is yet for an appointed time, but at the end it shall speak, and not lie: though it tarry, wait for it; because it will surely come, it will not tarry." (Habakkuk 2:1-3)

Many, many years He burned this scripture into my heart. I did not know, except that I knew it was from God and one day He would make real to me what the vision was. Down through the years He added a few scriptures. *"Is it not yet a very little while and Lebanon shall become a fruitful field and the fruitful field shall be esteemed as a forest."* (Isaiah 29:17) Then He gave other scriptures.

"Behold I do a new thing and even now it shall spring forth; shall ye not know it? I will make a way in the wilderness, and rivers in the desert… To give drink to My people, My chosen. This people have I formed for Myself; they shall shew forth My praise." (Isaiah 43:19-21)

Pretty bold, isn't it? *"They shall shew forth My praise."*

Years and years these scriptures burned inside of me.

God called me to minister by His Spirit. I did not know about the baptism of the Holy Ghost. I did know Jesus – I had Him in my heart, in my life, I knew how to be led by Him and I knew these words came from Him. I knew they were a part of my life. Many years went by, and He called me. He called me to Africa to be a missionary. When He called me I was very excited. I was ready to take the whole world for Jesus! Oh, I was ready to go! Only He wasn't ready for me to go, and I wasn't really ready to go. I thought I was. After all, He called me, so I was ready to go.

Then one day I was ironing clothes. I was standing at that ironing board and I said, "Lord, if You've called me, then I need to go." He said, "Agnes, it took Me forty years to train Moses in Pharaoh's court." I said, "Forty years, Lord?" He paused for a minute and He said, "It took Me forty years on the backside of the desert." I said, "God, eighty years?" That's exactly what I said to Him. Then I said, "Lord, if its eighty years, then eighty years it will be." And right at that moment, I settled it in my heart that God had charge of my life, about Africa and everything else. I just settled it right there with the Lord, and I never asked Him again.

One day a pastor spoke to me and he said, "Agnes, whatever God permits to come into your life from this moment forward, you take it as a part of the preparation for the call, the work that God has called you to do." Eighty years, that's what He said. So I wasn't to be any different from Moses. I was to be trained.

I was on the East Coast and God brought me to the West Coast, and guess where? On the desert – I had not been in California very long. I came in 1943, and in 1954, He set me on this land. He said, "This is My sanctuary, and this is where you'll be." Little did I know it would be forty years, except when I remembered what He said to me it was forty years on the desert for Moses.

From the time that the Lord called me, God began to change my life. Amen. When we have our confidence in Him, and we put our trust in Him, then we can depend on Him, and He will bring to pass that which concerns us. So I never grew weary of His training. It was not easy, because God had to do for me what He has to do for everybody else. He has to take out of us the traditions, and bondages, and all the things that we accumulate all our lives and was handed down from generation to generation. He has to take it out of us, so He can fill us with Himself, His love, His peace, His joy, His righteousness. He gave me a scripture: Ezekiel 1, 2 and 3. Ezekiel 1 was the Revelation of Jesus Christ to Ezekiel – a mighty revelation of Jesus. And Jesus has revealed Himself to us as the mighty Christ the Giver of life – the Giver of our life. And He brings us to the place in Him where we can also share that which is given to others.

"The Vision That Tarried No Longer Tarries"

One day the Lord told me, "The vision that tarried no longer tarries, it's here." You know when He told that to me? 1967. Anybody recall what happened in 1967? I think it was probably June of 1967. We had the Six-Day war in Israel. He said, "The vision no longer tarries, it's here."

In 1954, I was living in the Tujunga area, and I asked the Lord a simple question. Lord, do you want us to buy property here? And He spoke to me by the Word. He said, *"Is it not yet a little while and Lebanon shall become a fruitful field, and the fruitful field shall be esteemed as a forest?* I said, "God, what does that have to do with what I asked You? He said, "Go and read Isaiah 58." So, as I dried my hands, and walked from my kitchen into my living room, the Spirit of Revelation came upon me. I never experienced anything like it. It felt like my mind was moved out of the way, and the Spirit of the Lord came and began to unfold this word to me.

As I began to read, He unfolded it.

1. Cry aloud, spare not, lift up thy voice like a trumpet, and shew my people their transgression, and the house of Jacob their sins.

2. Yet they seek Me daily, and delight to know My ways, as a nation that did righteousness, and forsook not the ordinance of their God: they ask of Me the ordinances of justice; they take delight in approaching God.

3. Wherefore have we fasted, say they, and thou seest not? Wherefore have we afflicted our soul, and thou takest no knowledge? Behold, in the day of your fast ye find pleasure, and exact all your labours.

4. Behold, ye fast for strife and debate, and to smite with the fist of wickedness: ye shall not fast as ye do this day, to make your voice to be heard on high.

5. Is it such a fast that I have chosen? A day for a man to afflict his soul? Is it to bow down his head as a bulrush, and to spread sackcloth and ashes under him? Wilt thou call this a fast, and an acceptable day to the LORD?

6. Is not this the fast that I have chosen? To loose the bands of wickedness, to undo the heavy burdens, and to let the oppressed go free, and that ye break every yoke? Is it not to deal thy bread to the hungry, and that thou bring the poor that are cast out to thy house? When thou seest the naked, that thou cover him; and that thou hide not thyself from thine own flesh?

7. Then shall thy light break forth as the morning, and thine health shall spring forth speedily: and thy righteousness shall go before thee; and the glory of the LORD shall be thy rereward.

8. Then shalt thou call, and the LORD shall answer; thou shalt cry, and He shall say, Here I Am. If thou take away from the midst of thee the yoke, the putting forth of the finger, and speaking vanity;

9. And if thou draw out thy soul to the hungry, and satisfy the afflicted soul; then shall thy light rise in obscurity, and thy darkness be as the noonday:

10. And the LORD shall guide thee continually, and satisfy thy soul in drought, and make fat thy bones: and thou shalt be like a watered garden, and like a spring of water, whose waters fail not.

11. And they that shall be of thee shall build the old waste places: thou shalt raise up the foundations of many generations; and thou shalt be called, the repairer of the breach, the restorer of paths to dwell in.

12. If thou turn away thy foot from the Sabbath, from doing thy pleasure on My holy day; and call the Sabbath a delight, the holy of the LORD, honourable; and shalt honor Him, not doing thine own ways, nor finding thine own pleasure, nor speaking thine own words:

13. Then shalt thou delight thyself in the LORD; and I will cause thee to ride upon the high places of the earth, and feed thee with the heritage of Jacob thy father: for the mouth of the LORD hath spoken it.

"Cry aloud, lift up thy voice like a trumpet, and shew My people their transgressions." Why does He use the word "shew" here? You could raise your voice, and let it sound like a trumpet, but it wouldn't necessarily show anybody anything. Would it? So there has to be a demonstration of what He's talking

about. *"Shew My people their transgression, and the house of Jacob their sins."*

Let's go back a little bit and let's look at the Christian world today.

Let's take the Jewish people for a minute. He's talking about His people, the Jews. They make long prayers, He said… and when Jesus came, and everywhere He went, the Pharisees, and the Sadducees, the hypocrites, and they all followed Him. But they only followed to criticize Him. *"They daily sought Him, they delighted to know His ways…"* What was the problem with the children of Israel down through the centuries? What was it? They did what they wanted to do: they did not do what God wanted them to do. Every once in a while God had to send them off into a strange country, because they weren't hearing what He was saying, and they were not doing it. So He sent them off into other countries, hoping they might tell the heathen about Him. But they didn't. So He says here, you're doing all of this you're still saying you're doing My will, and you aren't doing My will at all. You're saying you're a righteous nation and you're keeping God's ordinances but you're not at all.

Is His Church Doing His Will?

Here we are today. We all know these are the last days. I believe this is the last generation before Jesus comes. All things point to the coming of the Lord. But something has to take place in the Christian world before Jesus comes. He's talking about all the things they profess to do and to be, which they are not. He says you do all of this, but that's not what pleases me. He says this is not what I have chosen for you to do. Then comes all the denominations, and each denomination has a different theory, a different way. And they all build their castles. But Jesus said, "I am the way, I am the truth, I am the light, I am the life. No man can come up any other way." He's the Giver of life, but He has a way for us to go.

The Lord told me when He gave me the Revelation of Isaiah 58, He told me He was going to deal seriously, heavily, with every church that professed His name. All the doctrines of men, He was going to deal with. He said, "I am sending the Spirit of Truth, and as the Spirit of Truth comes, it's going to go into the churches, and the Spirit of Truth is going to speak. And if they hear it, they will receive the truth, but if they do not hear it, they will go into deception – never to come out of that deception. For God is moving today with the Spirit of Truth throughout the world. The Spirit of the Lord is pouring out upon all flesh everywhere in the world. He's not depending upon the church world, He's depending upon the power, and the glory, and the kingdom of Jesus Christ to take the Word by the Holy Ghost into the nations of the world. But He's preparing a people. These people He has chosen for Himself, and He's preparing that people that they would not be like the children of Israel. They will not be like people that profess to be Christians, but don't know Jesus. He said, "I'm going into the churches. I'm going to speak the truth by the Spirit of Truth." He said it's going to be so straight that nobody will be able to deny it – so mighty that no one would be able to stand up and say anything to God. Right here He is stripping from these people the pretense that they were following God. They weren't pleasing God.

"Behold I do a new thing," saith the Lord. "And shall ye not know it? I will make a way in the wilderness and rivers in the desert to give drink to My people, My chosen that I have formed for Myself." Isaiah 43:19-20b

He's forming us in His own likeness, in His own image. It's Jesus and nothing else. When He finished telling them what they were like, He said, *"It is such a fast that I have chosen?"* Then He said, *"Is not this the fast that I have chosen? To loose the bands of wickedness, to undo the heavy burdens and let the oppressed go free and that ye break every yoke?"* When you go into the churches today, do you see this power? Do you see it being done? Where are the people that need the help? There are a lot of them in the church, that's true, but there are a lot of them in the road. Nobody cares whether most of them out there are living or dying, hungry or no place to sleep. I believe with every fiber of my being that God has intended for this scripture to be the church's way of doing things. I believe it is God's way for His church.

You followed Jesus when He walked the earth. Where did He go? He met the needs of the people – where the people were. He has a church. It's a church without spot, it's a church without wrinkle and it's His body. But they're going to do what <u>He</u> wants them to do, and they're not going to be affected by the traditions and bondages of men. Remember one thing: the Spirit of the Lord gave me this by the Spirit of Revelation. Not by man's wisdom, or knowledge, or counsel, or direction, but by God Himself, He gave it to me according to his Word.

> "Is not this the fast that I have chosen? To loose the bands of wickedness, undo the heavy burdens and let the oppressed go free and that ye break every yoke?"

Then why are we not seeing it done today? You're not seeing it done in the churches too much. Now, I'm not against churches, I want you to know that, but I'm giving you the Word as God gave it to me. When His church rises and obeys Him, something mighty is going to happen in this world. He's getting His church ready. But we have to remember it's by the Spirit of the Lord, not any other way, according to His Word.

> "Is it not to deal thy bread to the hungry, and that thou bring the poor that are cast out to thy house? When thou seest the naked, that thou cover him: and that thou hide not thyself from thine own flesh?"

You see, when God gave us this Word, He gave it for this day. He didn't give it to me for 1954. He gave it to me for now. And this is why we have what we have in this place. This is why we obey the command of the Lord and this is why the Lord meets our needs – not man – <u>God</u> meets them.

> "Then shall thy light break forth as the morning, and thine health shall spring forth speedily; and thy righteousness shall go before thee; the glory of the LORD shall be thy rereward. Then shall thou call, and the LORD shall answer; thou shalt cry, and He shall say, Here I am…"

Why Are We Christians?

Why are we Christians? Why are we called by His name? That we might know Him and walk with Him and obey Him. Or are we doing it just to be called Christians? But He said, "If you do this, then your light shall be as the morning."

You know, I don't mind what other people do. I don't mind what other Christians do. But what I want more than anything else in this world is to know that when I call, God hears me and He answers me. Amen. It doesn't matter how somebody patterns their life. It doesn't matter how churches are formed. Jesus formed me, and I'm His church. He's in you, and you're the church. Amen. He said, "…when you call, I will answer."

Then He said, *"If thou take away from the midst of thee the yoke…"* What is the yoke that binds us? There are a lot of yokes? *"…the putting forth of the finger…"* What's that? Judging one another. *"…and speaking vanity;"* How many vain things do we speak continually?

Then put it away.

"And if thou draw out thy soul to the hungry, and satisfy the afflicted soul; then shall thy light rise in obscurity, and thy darkness be as the noon day:" We're not walking in this way alone. We're walking this way because it's God's way, and God is with us, Jesus is with us, and He ordained for us to go this way according to His Word. *"…thy darkness shall be as the noon day: And the LORD shall guide thee continually, and satisfy thy soul in drought, and make fat thy bones: and thou shalt be like a watered garden, and like a spring of water, whose waters fail not."*

I hear people say to me, "Oh, you have a 'helps' ministry." No I don't have a 'helps' ministry. I have everything God said for us to do. He's doing it! I didn't start this, God started it, and He's the One who's going to finish it. Amen.

How glorious it is when you walk with Him, and you know that He hears you, and you know that He's with you, and you know that He's going to finish the job that He's doing. Amen. If we'll obey Him. That's why we must be careful how you treat the provision that God give to you. God has a way that we must go to have His blessings, to have rivers of living water inside of us, and to be satisfied in drought. And out there are multitudes on the streets, multitudes that are hungry, and don't know Him, – the homeless – those that have bands of wickedness binding them and heavy burdens they cannot be free from – the oppressed cannot free themselves.

But the Lord will sift and clean us. He will sift and clean according to His Word – if we obey Him. People read this book, this chapter, and say, "Oh, that's on fasting." No. It's on obedience. Obedience! If we will do this, God will do this. If we don't do it, we can't expect God to do anything. I remember one day, after many years, when the Lord started sending me abundant amounts of food. But God trained us in it. He taught us how to sort out the bad and find some good. Even though in the beginning we ended up with a handful of good, we learned how to sort out the bad, and throw it away. We couldn't even feed it to the animals – we had to bury it.

I didn't know where we were going to get the food, but I obeyed the Lord, and the Lord told me: "You go into the markets, and you tell them what you are doing, and I will cause them to give unto you." When they got the courage enough to go and talk to the people in charge, God began to move on the hearts. We did not beg. We said, "This is what we're doing, we're obeying God, we're feeding the hungry," and God took care of it. He's still taking care of it, many years later. Amen.

We Must Be Trained

He said, *"They that shall be of thee shall build up the old waste places:"* Now the vision was not given just for local people. It was given for the whole world, and that's why He didn't give it until the end of time. If you know anything about the conditions of the world, they are all starving to death. Aren't they? God has a plan to pour out His Spirit upon all flesh, and He told me one time: "If I don't have it for you, I will create it for you." And I believe it. Amen. This Word never fails if we obey it. But we have to be obedient to Him. But if you are listening and by the Spirit of the Lord, He will train you in the way He wants you to go. But if you're not listening, then that's not His fault, that's yours. But He said, *"...they that shall be of thee shall build up the old waste places; shall raise up the foundations of many generations;..."*

He sent us into the villages in Africa, in India and in other parts of the world. He sent us when they were hundreds of years behind time, and they had nothing. He sent us there with the Gospel of Jesus Christ to feed the hungry, to clothe the naked, to give them something to live for and to give them hope. To be *"the restorer of paths to dwell in".*

Then He goes on to say, *"...if we turn away our feet from the Sabbath to do our own thing...if we will honor Him, not doing our own ways, nor finding our own pleasures, nor speaking our own words."*

When Jesus came, there were three things that He did. He did not come to find His own way. He came to go the way of the Father. He did not come to please Himself, but to please the Father. He did not come speaking His own words, but speaking the words of the Father. Jesus wants us so filled with Him that these three things shall become a part of our life, that you can't separate it from our daily walk – that we know this is what God has put within us that we, too, may do what He's called us to do. If you will do this, if you'll delight yourself in the Lord, He said, *"I will cause you to ride upon the high places of the earth."*

God has something moving. He has Ezekiel's wheel ready to take off. And the only people who are going to ride in that wheel are the people who are trained by the Spirit of the Living God. Not anybody else. We'd better be trained by the Spirit of the Lord, because he's getting ready to take off across this whole earth. We aren't going to go hungry while we're riding because while we're riding on the high places of the earth, He's going to feed us *"with the heritage of Jacob, thy father. For the mouth of the Lord hath spoken it."* Isaiah did not say it. God said it.

So your sure place is in Jesus Christ, who only does the will of the Father, only speaks what the Father speaks and does what God has called Him to do. No pleasure of His own, but to please the Father. *"For the mouth of the Lord hath spoken it."*

That's how positive it is.

If you don't believe it, that's fine with me, because I believe it. I believe every word of it because He's proved it. He said,

"Shew My people their transgressions." The church today is so jealous of what God is doing, but they won't do it themselves, and they are going to come up short, because they failed to hear what God is saying and do what God says. He said, *"Shew My people..."*

What is Sommer Haven doing? We are just obeying the Lord; to shew the people what God wants them to do. Amen. Do you hear it? If we will delight ourselves in the Lord, we will ride upon the high places of the earth. *"For the mouth of the Lord hath spoken it."*

God began this Training Center, God is in it, and God is going to finish it. It's the Lord that gave it to us, it's the Lord that's doing it, and it's the Lord that's getting the glory for it, and not man. We have to come the way of the Spirit of God and be trained by the Spirit of God, so that God can receive all the glory and man will be blessed by having let God have His way. *"Behold I do a new thing and even now it shall spring forth, and shall ye not know it. He'll make a way in the wilderness, and rivers in the desert to give drink to My people, My chosen – that I have formed for Myself, and they shall shew forth My praise."*

All we need to be concerned about is our obedience and allowing Him to have His way in our life. Let Him form us that we might be as He is in this world. It matters that we line up with God. The Word says He never fails, His Word never fails –<u>never</u> <u>fails</u>! Hallelujah!

We Only Have Time To Run!

So we give to you the Word of the Lord that you may take it, receive it, run with it and give it wherever the Lord sends you to give it. *"For the mouth of the Lord hath spoken it."* The vision no longer tarries. We don't have time to play around; we only have time to run. *"That they that run may read it as they run."* We only have time to put together what God has called us to do, and pick it up, and run with it, and give it all over the world where He's called us to go. He gave this vision that we might fulfill it according to His Word. And according to His Word, He is with us, He will be with us, and He will meet our every need. And He has done it: the impossible has been done in this Training Center because God is doing it and not us leaning on the arm of flesh, not us leaning on the almighty dollar, not us leaning on the people who have millions. That's their problem. We have God. Amen. We have Him.

I've never gone hungry in my life. Even during the depression I never went hungry. God picked me up from my hometown and set me down in Kentucky in a little school where they had plenty to eat. And He kept me there when the rest of my family were going through the soup line. Only because I honored Him and obeyed Him, I never went hungry in my life, because He's been my provider.

God loves us! That call, that vision, is still before us to run with it. We need to enjoy every minute that we're working with the Lord on these things and forget about our flesh and forget about the gripes, and give it to the Lord, and He will handle them. But run, because our time is short. We have a whole world to reach before Jesus comes, and He's pouring out His Spirit, so we need to get ready to run. The vision does not tarry. It shall come to pass, and it is coming to pass. It's coming to pass right on this land, right now – what God promised.

The Key Is Obedience

We're showing the people, no matter who they are, what God's way is and if they will do it, they will have the same blessings of God in their churches, with their people, if they obey God. If they don't obey Him, they won't have it. But one day they're going to stand before Him and He's going to open up the book and He's going to say,

> "I was hungry and you didn't feed me. I was naked and you didn't clothe Me. I was sick and you didn't visit Me. I was in prison and you didn't come to Me. Depart from Me you workers of iniquity." Matthew 25:42-43

It's not how great we are, but He was hungry, and we didn't feed Him. He was naked, and we didn't clothe Him. He was sick, and we didn't visit Him. He was in prison, and we didn't go to Him. They said, *"Lord, when saw we thee hungry?" "If you did it unto the least of these, you did it unto Me."* (Matthew 25:45) We can talk about every doctrine of men. We can talk about all these things, but here's the finale – the final thing before God: Did we do it?

The rest of it doesn't matter. It doesn't matter. It doesn't matter who we think we are. It matters who we think Jesus is, and let Him become the supreme ruler of our lives and watch Him do the impossible for us every moment of the day.

Closing Prayer

Father, we thank You for the Word. We thank You, Lord, that You've imparted it to each and every one of us, that we might hear it, and that we might obey it, and that we might show forth this which You have given unto us; that we might show to all Your people by the Spirit of the Lord the way that You would have each one to go. Lord, we thank You, that it's not by might, and it's not by power, but it's by Your Spirit. Lord, train each one of us by Your Spirit that we may walk in the way that You would have us to walk. That our pleasures would be to please You, our words shall be Your words, that we shall give to others if they may hear it, receive it and do it. God, I thank You for this Word. Let it ring inside of our every being, oh, God, and let us fulfill it according to this which pleases You. We give You glory. Mighty God, I ask You to open every one of our hearts, open our ears to hear, to receive, and to obey the Word of the Lord. God, we thank You that you've chosen us, that You might be exalted in all things, and for Your glory. In Jesus' Name, we ask it. Amen.

Holly Vanderberg and Agnes I. Numer

TRANSFIGURATION

Lord Jesus, we pray that you will quicken our hearts to receive that which you have for us that our lives will be transformed by the power of the resurrected Christ. Even this day, we ask you to do the creative miracles in each of us that are needed to bring us into that place with you. Direct our paths and lead us in the way you would have us to go. We give you glory and praise and honor this day, in your wonderful name we ask it. Amen.

We are excited about what God is doing in us. I had a call from Arizona and the Lord told me He was going to release His Shekinah glory on His people. I know this is true for it is time for the glory of the Lord to come; but we have to go to the mountain to receive him in His glory.

God brought the children of Israel out of Egypt and took them to Mount Sinai where He spoke to them and gave them life. But they were afraid and didn't want God to speak to them. They would rather hear through Moses. They chose Moses to be their leader rather than God.

God is calling us back to the mountain and the Lord will be the one that speaks to us; that His glory and presence shall be over us continually. This scripture is when Jesus took the three disciples with him up into a high mountain.

> Matthew 17:1 And after six days Jesus taketh Peter, James, and John his brother, and bringeth them up into an high mountain apart. 2 And was transfigured before them: and his face did shine as the sun, and his raiment was white as the light. 3 And, behold, there appeared unto them Moses and Elias talking with him. 4 Then answered Peter, and said unto Jesus, Lord, it is good for us to be here: if thou wilt, let us make here three tabernacles; one for thee, and one for Moses, and one for Elias. 5 While he yet spake, behold, a bright cloud overshadowed them: and behold a voice out of the cloud, which said, This is my beloved Son, in whom I am well pleased; hear ye him. 6 And when the disciples heard it, they fell on their face, and were sore afraid. 7 And Jesus came and touched them, and said, Arise, and be not afraid. 8 And when they had lifted up their eyes, they saw no man, save Jesus only. 9 And as they came down from the mountain, Jesus charged them, saying, Tell the vision to no man, until the Son of man be risen again from the dead. Matthew 17:1

We saw when the children of Israel went up into Mount Sinai where God spoke to them and they didn't die, they lived. They chose to have God with them and to talk to them. They chose to have Moses do the ministry to them.

Now God is calling us back into a relationship with Him. Here Jesus was on this mountain where He was transformed before them. Peter says, "Let us build three tabernacles." A voice came from heaven and said, "This is my beloved Son, in whom I am well pleased…"

The Lord is calling His body, His church, into that relationship with him that we might know him in the power of His resurrection, His kingdom and His glory. They saw the glory of the Father on the mountain where Jesus took them. They saw the glory of God; they saw the glory on Jesus right before them.

We need to see Jesus and Jesus only and recognize that He is the gospel. Anything other than Christ isn't the gospel. Hear him and don't get involved with everything else. Christ is the answer; He is the gospel! We need more of His presence; more of what He requires of us and know that He is in charge.

I was reading a little out of the book by E. Stanley Jones and he was talking about India. I find this true all over the world today as we have gone as missionaries and we have gone representing organizations and not going purely representing Jesus. The people thought we came to bring them western religion and they don't want it.

If we bring Jesus, they will accept Jesus, but leave the rest of it off. I was reading this book. It's Christ of the India Road. How much I realized, being in those countries, that Christ is the only one that's going to be able to do what this world needs today. There is no other way that these things are going to be done except allowing Christ in us to arise and to allow Him to take us to Mt. Sinai. And allow him to strip us of all of these things so that when we come before Him we can be filled with His kingdom, power and glory.

He is getting ready to bring His church into a position that is going to throw a light against this old sin cursed world. But He has to use us for He has no one else!

They stood there on this beautiful mountain with Moses and Elijah. Moses had his day bringing the law; and the prophets had their day; but now Jesus has His day. He is going to arise in His people and they are going recognize Him and take every tradition out of ministry.

Peter wanted to hold onto the law and prophets; but God said,

> This is my beloved Son in whom I am well pleased. Luke 9:35

God wants to make us as Jesus was when He walked the earth so that He can entrust us with the kingdom.

The Lord said,

> Arise, shine for thy light has come and the glory of the Lord is risen ... Isaiah 60:1

We must go before him and let him strip us of all the bondages that have been ours. We might think these things are fine; maybe they were in the last generation but they aren't now. I am excited about what God is doing today and what Jesus wants to do in us. He wants to bring His power and glory through us.

Even in the mountain when He was transfigured before them He let them see Moses and Elijah; but the Father said, "This is my beloved Son in whom I am well pleased; hear ye him." He wants us to enter into that place in him where we can allow Christ to be the center of our life. Where He is in us and we can see the glorious things that He is about to do on the earth today.

We find in the Word where it says,

> For, behold, the darkness shall cover the earth, and gross darkness the people: Isaiah 60:3

People are getting so gross with the garbage and stuff that it is unbearable. The church has been asleep and complacent following the traditions of men. Ten million Americas didn't go to the polls to vote in the last election; what are we doing. We are giving place for the enemy. We have to take back America for God through intercession; by allowing Christ to come forth in us and shaking off everything else. We need to realize God wants to use America in this world to bring about this awakening, which must come through Jesus and none other.

I'm realizing inside myself that God is viewing strange and mighty things; we need to be ready for them. I expect the children to shake off the junk that's around them just as I expect the adults to do the same thing and allow the Lord to arise in us and change our lives. We aren't going anywhere unless we do; because the darkness and gross darkness will prevent this hope of glory arising upon us. Unless Christ is in control of our lives we aren't going survive in this world of terror and horror. Jesus is the only way!

We are living in perilous times; but we are living when Jesus wants us to have a full revelation of Him glory. He wants to give us the fullness of His Spirit to change a world that needs to know him.

I think of India so much because I have been there many times. That nation would have been won to Jesus. I think of Japan when Mc Arthur was there and took over Japan and asked for ten thousand missionaries from every church in America to be sent and only two responded. We can't be complacent, we have to arise. We have to allow God to reveal His son to us and Christ will reveal The Father to us.

We can't become complacent; we have to arise and allow the Son of Righteousness to come forth in us with healing in his wings; that we may go forth and bring the light that is needed in this dark world today. We need to go to the mountain where Jesus is and surrender our life to him. We must decrease as He increases until He has charge of our life. Through the flow of His spirit we can get a lot accomplished. He has called us to grow up; we have to lose sight of our self and see Jesus only.

Some of us have families and husband and wives. If we line up with Gods order the Holy Ghost will move. If we line up with God, He will move with husband and wife and the flow will come that nothing can separate because Jesus is in control. As long as we try to keep the control we will go the way of complacency and He won't be able to use us. You might think this is pretty straight. It is, straight from him! It's not from me. You need to lay down the hindrances.

I'd like to read Isaiah 60. Maybe you're not aware that the whole world is open for the gospel. You don't know Jesus has only given us a short time to do these miracles that He has put before us. Maybe you don't know that, but I do! We need to get out of our flesh and let God use us to the fullest extent.

> Isaiah 60:1 Arise, shine; for thy light is come, and the glory of the LORD is risen upon thee. 2 For, behold, the darkness shall cover the earth, and gross darkness the people: but the LORD shall arise upon thee, and his glory shall be seen upon thee. 3 And the Gentiles shall come to thy light, and kings to the brightness of thy rising. 4 Lift up thine eyes round about, and see: all they gather themselves together, they come to thee: thy sons shall come from far, and thy daughters shall be nursed at *thy* side. 5 Then thou shalt see, and flow together, and thine heart shall fear, and be enlarged; because the abundance of the sea shall be converted unto thee, the forces of the Gentiles shall come unto thee. Isaiah 60:1-5

It means multitudes of people. What are we going to do with multitudes of people? It will come as we allow the Lord to take His place in us. I'm very excited in what He is doing in Montana and Asia and Japan. The doors are being opened; but where are the people we are going to send? We have to allow him to take His place in us. We have to allow God to train us. If He is in charge, He will train us.

When you get on the mission field, you will wish you had more training. You must be trained the way Jesus wants to train you. The door into Japan and China is open. They don't know Christ; they don't know Jesus. But only through the revelation of Jesus can this world be changed. I am persuaded that God isn't finished with this world. I understand this is not what a lot of people teach. I'm not trying to teach the doctrines of men; this is what the Lord says.

We give God the glory for the shaking and we have to line up with Jesus. Let the Lord come forth in each one, not to go backward but forward in him. We have a lot before us; but the Lord is the answer. We have seen some mighty miracles happen here more and more.

I am aware that there is a momentum to take this kingdom, of His righteousness, to the ends of the earth. He has placed within us His righteousness that the world might know who Jesus is. I know when God pours out His glory they won't be able to resist it. We can't resist it or we will go back into darkness.

Jesus is counting on us to die to ourselves that He may live. We have to decrease that He might increase. We will be able to stand, because He is sending us. We must arise in him and let His kingdom come forth in us, so that His gospel can be preached in "all" the world.

When Gideon had his big army, you wonder why he had to make it only 300. It is because man can't do it himself, He has to trust God to do it. We can't do anything! We have to let God arise within us and change us and allow His Spirit to move through us. The enemy wants to divide us into groups; but God wants us to come forth to move as one as He works through us.

The children on Mt. Sinai made a choice to hear God through Moses instead of directly. God will not let me interfere with people making choices. Many people ask questions; but I tell them they have to make that decision for themselves. We have to allow him to come forth in us so that He can move through us, that the world can know Jesus.

We need to get things in order that we can give Jesus to the nations of the world. We must know that all the things He is developing for the 3rd world are so they can run through their own country with the gospel that will change their people. Let God put our shoulders to the plow and not look back. We have to move forward.

I sat at a table last night and I heard comments others were making about money. I praise the Lord I don't have to handle the money; the Lord does it. We give him glory and we praise him. If we could only realize what He has placed in our hands and what He requires of us. Let Jesus be Jesus in us. He will do everything right and He will give us of His kingdom, power and glory; that the world might know who He is. This gospel of the kingdom shall be preached in "all" of the world as a witness to all nations and then the end shall come.

I have heard people make remarks that the gospel has gone all over the world; but it isn't true. That is just somebody's perception. It must go to the ends of the earth.

I believe it is God's glory filling the people; He is waiting so that He can send us to all nations; but it's up to us. He is moving very quickly now. Remember, it is up to us.

> But unto you that fear my name shall the Sun of righteous arise with healing in His wings; and ye shall go forth, and grow up as calves of the stall. Malachi 4:2

How long do you allow a calf to be in a stall? Not too long! You open up the gate and let it go out. It grows up all at once.

Let God be Jesus in us. "This is my beloved Son in whom I am well pleased." It is Jesus and we must hear him. He must arise in us then we have a job to do.

The devil is sure he has us in his hands; he is sure God's people are going to be in his hands. God is going to have the world in His hand and He is coming for a church without wrinkle. Go to that mountain and burn out the stuff in our lives. I'm excited about it. I'm sure God has given me an insight into it. The kingdom that Satan took away, Jesus is gathering it to give it back to the Father.

What happens when Jesus presents it back to the Father? Christ, himself, is always under subjection. After He had finished, He gave it to the Father with great humility. We have a great Savior! In submitting to God and Christ we have the privilege to watch and to be a part of it. Jesus becomes everything to us. Amen.

Agnes I. Numer and Joseph Thomas

UNDER NEW MANAGEMENT

You can forget the things of the past and go forth praising and thanking God. The Lord just helps us so much, to grow in him and appreciate him. The Spirit of the Lord gave life to me and I began to realize it. The enemy wants to control us and I got to thinking how the Lord gave us life. We hesitate because it is so awesome when you are realizing it is God and it is our heavenly Father, it is the Holy Spirit that are abiding within us. We just have to remember that He is doing the work in our lives

I know one time when I first got saved I was having a hard time. I had 5 younger brothers and sisters I had to raise and 3 older than myself and my father. I was just a little child. I'm not very tall now. The work was very far from what I could think of doing. I would get discouraged and I would want to give up. It was too much with my sassy brothers and sisters. They would say, "You can't tell me what to do." I would get so discouraged that I would go upstairs and get down on my knees before God and cry out before Him: "How can I be a

Christian for you when I have to contend with all these things?" He said, "You are like a little child learning to walk. A child always gets up and keeps on trying until they're strong enough to walk on their own."

That's the way it is with the Lord. We have to lean on him and trust him. When we do, when we need help to encourage us He is there to give whatever we need. I praise God that He doesn't expect us to be something we're not. Older Christians look at you expect you to shoot up all at once, to mature all at once; but that isn't so. As we take the word He brings life to us. There are some things that are very vital for our understanding.

> *There is* therefore now no condemnation to them which are in Christ Jesus, who walk not after the flesh, but after the Spirit. 2 For the law of the Spirit of life in Christ Jesus hath made me free from the law of sin and death. Romans 8:1-2

When we become a new creation in Christ Jesus there was a new law placed in us that was to have control in our life: the law of Christ Jesus.

> For what the former law could not do, in that it was weak through the flesh, God sending His own Son in the likeness of sinful flesh, and for sin, condemned sin in the flesh: 4 That the righteousness of the law might be fulfilled in us, who walk not after the flesh, but after the Spirit. Romans 8:3-4

When we accept Christ and He comes to live in us, we are a new creation. There is a new law for us and that law is the spirit of life in Christ Jesus. The law of life of Christ Jesus is in us and the old law of sin and death is destroyed. When we accept him and go to the cross and our sins are forgiven, we are washed in the blood of the lamb and we come before him and He baptizes us. When we are baptized in water the old man goes down and is buried in that water and he doesn't come up any more! We are then a new creature with a new life in Christ Jesus and He enables us to be what He wants us to be.

There is a new law, the law of the spirit! This is why it is so important for us to walk in the Spirit of God. The law of the flesh destroys; but the law of the spirit gives life. The Lord gives life to us; but the enemy comes and tries to snatch it. Remember, we are under new management: Christ is us! He will enable us to do what He wants us to do. The law of the Spirit of Life in Christ Jesus says it has made us free to walk in the spirit, move in the spirit and obey the Spirit of God.

This new law has full control over our life and you can tell the devil and the flesh to go. We are under new ownership; we have a new owner over our life. We don't have to be controlled by the flesh or by the devil. A new law has come into our life and the law of the spirit has made us free and removed all of that old stuff out of our life. It has given us joy and peace, righteousness and all the things that come with God within us. You don't battle with the devil, you kick him out. You kick out the flesh and you start walking and allowing the law of the spirit to have control. It's not difficult to decide to let God do it. We have to make the decision.

When we decide we want the law of the Spirit of Life we are set free and the law of sin and death has no more control over us. Go Satan! Go flesh! We are going to let the Spirit of Life reign in us by Christ Jesus. As we do this the enemy doesn't hang around. We begin to thank God that we have a new law. It is so wonderful! The Bible says there is no law against love, peace, joy, and righteousness. We have it inside of us and they can't take it away; the devil can't take it away. We are no longer bound; we are loosened by Jesus.

Christ Jesus in us is the hope of glory. Christ in us is what we need to know and say, "We aren't struggling in our flesh, we are walking by the Spirit of God; we are walking the way God wants us to walk." We are going to have hindrances; but nothing is going to stop us. We know who owns us and we are going through what we are going through. We don't have to be afraid. We can put our hands in His with confidence that Christ lives in us and a new law is operating there: the law of liberty! We are no longer bound by the things of darkness but we are set free.

Paul asked if anything can separate us from the love of God. He says that in all of these things we are more than conquers.

> Romans 8:35 Who shall separate us from the love of Christ? *shall* tribulation, or distress, or persecution, or famine, or nakedness, or peril, or sword? 36 As it is written, For thy sake we are killed all the day long; we are accounted as sheep for the slaughter. 37 Nay, in all these things we are more than conquerors through him that loved us. 38 For I am persuaded, that neither death, nor life, nor angels, nor principalities, nor powers, nor things present, nor things to come, 39 or height, nor depth, nor any other creature, shall be able to separate us from the love of God, which is in Christ Jesus our Lord. Romans 8:35-39

The solid gospel of Jesus Christ in us is the foundation that is laid in Christ. He said nothing shall separate us from the love of God. When the problems come and the enemy comes, we need to take hold of this fact: nothing is going to take that love of Christ from us. They might put you in prison and do all kinds of things to you. They may even take your life; but they can't take his peace, or his righteousness, or his holiness from us. There's no law in the land that can forbid us to have Christ in us if we purpose to let Christ reign in our heart and life. No circumstance can defeat us if we are determined to have this new management come forth in us

If we allow the Lord to come forth in our life, nothing can hinder us once we get this solid foundation inside of us. The joy of the Lord becomes our strength and the love of God in us becomes such a force that nothing the enemy does matters and nothing can take that strength away from us. Nothing can separate us from His love! In these days we need to be rooted and grounded more and more. We need to know him in such power that nothing can separate us from His love, His peace, His joy, His righteousness and His holiness.

If we allow Him to take His place in us and as we allow Him to take His place in us, a new law comes into effect in our lives. The law is God in Christ Jesus and it has made us free from the law of sin and death. Because when we flow by the Spirit of God you don't have conflict. When we move the direction of God's Spirit we have rest and won't struggle with it.

This is one thing we have stress from the beginning: that we allow the Lord to flow through us and we can weather the storms. We might feel a few winds; but remember: it is not the flesh that is going to win as we allow Him to just take our life.

It is remarkable that we can live in a place like this, in peace and unity in God's Spirit. It is a miraculous thing that we can flow together and do what God wants us to do. It is so amazing what is accomplished here with so few people. It has to be Go; it can't be man! As we praise him and allow him to come in by His Spirit it is the demonstration of the gospel. In the middle of it you have people that might not be so easy to work with but he Spirit of the Lord is doing it. There might be winds but it will calm down and out of it comes the peace of God.

I never forget when the Lord first started me here, before I had the training center, and only one man was there at that time, I had a Russian friend come and she is going north. She said, "Agnes come and go with me." So I was intending to go; but I didn't ask the Lord. When we were fixing a pot of stew all at once a spot of that stew got on my floor and I slipped. How you can fall in that kitchen is strange because there is no room to fall? I fell and broke a bone in my foot and one in hand. So I had to have a cast for 6 weeks. I forgot to ask God if He wanted me to go. He stopped me and I couldn't go. They had to have come in and help me. It was in January and it was very cold.

A man called me and said, "Sister Numer, we are having a convention and we need a place for some of our people to stay. Here I just came out of a cast and I didn't know how to walk and I wasn't too chipper about it but the Lord spoke to me. I said I will pray about it. He didn't wait 5 minutes and he called me back and said, "They are here. Have you decided what you are going to do?" The Lord told me to do it. I said, "Yes, Lord."

It was a hippie family with bare feet a runny nose. Here I am my house is cold, not ready for company; but the Lord said do it anyway. Before we knew it we had 25 people here. This one man came and stayed for 2 days and had no way out of the valley so he had to stay. There was no way he could get away. The Russian woman was expecting her 4th child and here they come. This hippie couple with the bare feet stayed for 3 months. Then the people from Morris Cerullo's ministry, and there was a man from Michigan, and from Texas; they began to come. That was the beginning. I thank God for the first man who was there in the beginning.

I remember our little girl, she comes in and there were people already there, and she asked "What are these people doing here?"

"God told me to bring these people" I said, that's alrighty. Another woman brought someone, and we had people everywhere. We had no trailers. The Lord sent the people. I was amazed at how the Lord works.

There was this Russian lady with 3 boys and this hippie couple with the runny noses and bare feet. She was so upset that this baby looked like this. Then comes my friend from Michigan and she was a wonderful cook; but there was friction. But I saw the Lord work. Every time and they would apologize and ask to be forgiven. I watched the Lord dissolve the things and then I began to understand what the Lord was doing.

We had beds everywhere. I had 3 beds in my room and I gave up my bedroom. We saw the Lord begin in such a way that man couldn't say they did it. God did it! We had no money; but the Lord supplied. This was before we started a training center. The Lord began to put the people with us. I wouldn't know, they even knew one another. The Spirit of the Lord would know them. They would come in from all over the United States. It was so beautiful and we never went hungry. That was a miracle.

When moving by the Spirit of the Lord, just do what He wants you to do. Don't forget, one woman must have had 7 or 8 in her car and we already had that many in our house. Why were that many in our house? She couldn't understand why there were so many people. I didn't try to figure it out because the Lord told me we might go out or in, and He might send them to me from all over the world.

It is this law of the spirit of life in Christ Jesus, which changes our lives so that we can flow together by the Spirit of the Lord, and it is His love, that can bind us together. Wherever we go in the world, they are going to know it is His love that has changed us. I know that it is His love that is stronger than anything in the whole world; stronger than the principalities and powers, and brings us into the love of Christ Jesus.

I praise him for the love of God in Christ Jesus and for the word that He has spoken. What He says, He will do. The changes that He will make, He will make; but He will make free in Christ Jesus from the law of sin and death. It is very mighty. Amen.

Take hold of it hold, don't let anything shake your faith or remove that love that God has put there. There are a lot of people on the streets that are homeless which we feed. We keep giving out hot dogs and we keep getting them in by the case. It looks like we aren't giving it out, there is so much. It is absolutely wonderful! This is what he wants to give His people.

Friday night a friend was weeping, she goes out and feeds the people in Los Angeles, and they were cold. She asked, "Do you have more than one blanket? Would you give them?" Then God moves and gives this bountiful blessing and some feed those people twice a day. They cook the food for them and God blesses it. In Jesus name we pray. Amen.

Agnes I. Numer - India circa 1977

Agnes I Numer, Sarai Jeffrey and Bro VA Joseph of India

UNDER NEW MANAGEMENT

Agnes I. Numer and Rev. Gnana Prakasam

Rev. Gnana Prakasam's Wife, Lilly (R) and Daughter, Mercy Gladys (Sweety) (L) continue the school and ministry to needy children today. All Nations International director, Teresa Skinner center. (ANI founded by Agnes I. Numer)

WAITING UPON THE LORD

The Lord is not going to be able to use us in the manner that He wants to unless we come into the full stature of Christ. We have to wait upon Him and learn His ways. We have to be disciplined and walk in step with God's will and His way and His timing; allowing the Lord to change us by His Spirit. He is bringing us into the full manifestation of God and releasing His power within us to the degree that we allow Him to have full control of our life. If we permit the Lord to train us, and are willing to wait on him, we will know that God has done certain things.

There are several things that we have to be brought into as we wait upon the Lord. One of them is that He releases power within us and its manifestation more than we have ever experienced. How far do you want to go? Are you willing to press forward in the spirit until you have reached the full statue of Christ and have God's power released in you? Are you willing to follow Christ's example and position yourself spiritually?

The disciple isn't above his master but any one that is perfect shall be as his master. One of the major keys to the supernatural order of God in Jesus' life was that He understood God's timing and walked in it. He didn't act on His own but received His instructions from the Father.

> Verily, verily, I say unto you, The Son can do nothing of himself, but what he seeth the Father do: for what things soever he doeth, these also doeth the Son likewise. John 5:19

He is saying that timing is the key to harvest. We want to rush ahead of God and do it our own way. We must walk in God's way and His timing, not our own. When we don't allow God to do this with us then we can't come into the maturity that He has for us. When we make our own decisions and use our own timing instead of God's, we set ourselves up for defeat.

The reason there is so much confusion in the church today is that many ministers and Christian leaders have failed to wait on God. I believe that God is moving us into places such as we have not witnessed before. We can't do anything except we do it His way and in His timing. He is bringing us into the full stature of Christ. If we are not asking God to add to us His faith, and if we are not allowing Him to process us, then we can't come into the fullness of God's love. We can't expect to go out in the power of His Spirit if our own ways and our own will are involved!

If we don't learn timing in the natural how will we learn it in the spiritual? If we can't take our time to do what is needed, we can't be disciplined in the way God wants it. Isn't it important for us to be on time instead of getting there in the middle of what the Lord is saying?

We need you be on time. Some say, "It doesn't matter if I am a half hour late for this or that." What if God is fine tuning us? Some are taking it as though we have no pressure put on us to keep the rules, so we observe our own rules. We feel a certain way, so we do it.

That isn't the way God wants us to do it. It is God's plan and there isn't a lot of pressure if we flow with Him. We don't have a lot of the pressure that people have when they are on jobs. We have a leisurely atmosphere and we have peace if we listen and flow with it. We can have our way if it isn't contrary to His Spirit. It still means we need to let Him have His way because He is bringing us into the full stature of Christ: God's will, God's way, God's timing! I know a lot of times we have to suffer through it. We don't feel good about going through it but what is God's purpose?

I remember when I was in the second year of college. I knew God had put me there for He had made a way for me to go. I came up to my second year and I took rheumatic fever. The President of the college came into my room and said, "This is one of the hardest things I have had to do; but due to the nature of your illness, we are going to have to put you in the hospital." I prayed and all of the people were praying for me in the school. It seemed that God didn't hear me. I felt like my faith was hanging by a thread and it was ready to break. My roommate Dorothy was backslidden. I said "Dorothy does God ever take you so far and forget you?" She said, "Agnes I'm not where I have been with the Lord; but one thing I know "He doesn't do that."

The Lord said "Agnes how important are souls to you?" I said, "Lord you know I would give my life." "Would you be willing to lie on the flat of your back for months for the sake of souls?" I said "Lord, forgive me for doubting the wisdom of your ways." They took me into a place in that hospital and I was in that bed 4 ½ months. My bed couldn't be put down because my heart might stop. I had to have my bed straight up at night. I asked one of the nurses if she would please put my bed down. She didn't know I wasn't allowed to have my bed down so she puts it down. The head nurse walks by, and grabs that thing, and puts it up as fast as she could, and she really balled her out.

Now I shouldn't have asked her to do it but I was tired of sitting up and wanted to lie down. All kinds of things happened it wasn't a picnic. I was critically ill and only God kept me alive and the pain was not so easy, but I finally realized that God had a plan that was greater than any plan that I could have thought of.

There were young men at that college that had the call of God on them. They were in stubbornness and were fighting against the call of God. While I lay peaceable in that bed the Lord poured the intercession in me and was breaking down the strong holds of the enemy in those young people's lives.

They had a revival that shook that place because God was able to pour through me the intercession that changed their lives. It wasn't easy. They called me the ray of sunshine. They had this huge hospital, and people came from all areas to see me, but it was God that was doing it. All kinds of things happened but God raised us up. Never was I able to go back to that school; instead we traveled for a month from the east coast to west coast. God brought me to California.

That was His plan, it wasn't mine. After I was here I had a lot of things happen that any one of them could have cost me my life; but God was doing something. I was never supposed to have any children. I had two children, but I went into heart failure, and we all survived. Six months after I was in California I was in bed and couldn't get up. Through it all God taught me. I didn't dictate to God how to do it or what I wanted to do.

I went through heavy persecution and accusations but I had to face it. If we are willing to let God process our life He will do it His way but we have to resign our will and allow Him to do it.

When you are ready for God to do the processing you may not have 80 years like I had. But time isn't the point; it is obedience, discipline and waiting upon the Lord. We are going to be able to allow His Spirit to flow through us if we can travail, intercede, and praise Him. God is going to send us out like when He sent our praise leader to the Philippines. Very few people knew what she went through all those months; it was very bad. But God had a reason for it and it did something in her life that nothing else could do.

The devil comes to make us sick and hinder us from what God wants us to have. We must be careful that we are not giving in to the works of the enemy. We have to do what God wants, and we have to be able to know what is of God, and what is of the enemy. I believe he does a high attack on this place to try to disrupt the flowing together in the training of the Lord, and we have to be able to stand against it.

I tell you for years the battle was bad in my body because the enemy was determined that I wasn't going to do what God wanted me to do; I was determined that I was. I said to the devil, "We aren't going to let you put tiredness on me. I'm going to get up and I got up out of that bed and shook the devil off. I won't use the word around here. I know the devil wants to do it.

There are a lot of things that are tactics of the devil. We need to know when the Lord is working with us so that we can be patient and not upset or disturbed. The only way that God can change us inwardly is going through these things. When I died on the operating table, I went up into the heavens and I saw the Lord face to face. He told me that the devil would try to take my life but I was in the palm of His hand and no man could take me out of it. The devil has tried it and people have tried it. They have said, "You are not of God" and all kinds of stuff; but I remember that the Lord said I am in the palm of His hand therefore no man can pluck me out. I have never erred from it because I know that God called me to lead the people out into the maturity of Christ, into the full stature in Him; to be trained by Him so that we can learn to wait upon the Lord and hear His voice and walk in His way and timing.

When God gave me Isaiah 58 I had the word many years before He brought it to pass. I had to wait for it because everybody said that woman is crazy; that stuff will never work. It has worked and it will come to pass and God is true with His word. We know if we will patiently wait on the Lord He will direct us according to His will. We won't be out of tune and we will know what God's way is and then we will walk in it. If we hinder the Lord then we can't do what He wants us to do.

I know that it is time to come into the full stature of Christ if we are willing to put aside our own way and let God have His. God will do what He wants to do and we can't rush it. Jesus waited on the timing of the Father. We are out of God's will if we fail to wait upon Him and we bring unnecessary pain and suffering upon ourselves and others.

We get tempted to give up and bring ourselves to a point of frustration and make ourselves vulnerable to Satan's attacks. In the beginning when we come to the Lord and we feel the zeal of the Lord, we think we are ready to go but we aren't. God is just giving us a taste of what it means to let us flow in His anointing.

I don't want to discourage anybody; but we need to be ready to run. God is preparing us. In order to run we have to come under the timing of the Lord in preparation of what God wants to do in our life. You might think you are ready and have the anointing but if God hasn't schooled us the enemy will trip us up. He gave them a command. He didn't go until He gave the command to go. If they hadn't given the command they wouldn't have been victorious they would have suffered defeat. They brought the release of God's power is waiting upon God.

To wait upon God means for us position ourselves spiritually so we are aligned with His plan. When we are aligned with His plan we must know what His plan is. When an individual waits upon God he is in his present position awaiting further instruction from God. What do I do next? What road do you want me to take next?

I know that waiting on God isn't a passive thing. He does not sit with his hands folded doing nothing; it involves seasons of prayer, spending time in the word, exercising spiritual discernment.

Releasing faith is waiting with a purpose in mind expecting God to give a specific instruction and guidance to anything in our circumstances. He said next week He is going to show how to wait upon Him and how vital it is for you to be able to have God's power flowing straight to you empowering you: a super natural power in Jesus. It is a major key.

Those that learn how to wait on God will have the supernatural flow of God released in them and they will have the call of almighty God upon their lives and an explanation within them that will enable them to endure the hardship and make them victorious over every obstacle that the enemy may place in their way. When everyone around them is fainting or falling by the road side those that are waiting on God will have the supernatural released within them that will enable them; that will let them go as far as they need to go.

How far do you want to go? Wait on God in all things. Our God loves you and you are blessed. You will keep on running and running. God told me the day would come that I would be running and there would be no way to stop.

People come through these doors from all parts of the world and we teach them. We have had a sample of this this week. Off they go with it to all parts of the world. They off doing their own thing and they aren't going very far.

If we are allowing Him to take out of us the things of the flesh He will have us ready to go out.

> I will stand upon my watch, and set me upon the tower, and will watch to see what he will say unto me, and what I shall answer when I am reproved. 2 And the LORD answered me, and said, Write the vision, and make *it* plain upon tables, that he may run that readeth it. 3 For the vision *is* yet for an appointed time, but at the end it shall speak, and not lie: though it tarry, wait for it; because it will surely come, it will not tarry. Habbabkuk 2:1-3

He is preparing us to run with the word. He is using Isaiah 58 and all the other scriptures in the word of God to bring us into the full stature of Jesus Christ so that He can flow through us to do the will of the Father and go the way the Father would have us go to go.

I have seen things happening when I went to other countries for I was going exactly in the timing of the Lord. Wherever we were going we would meet ertain people and it flows in God's timing.

The truth must be in us and become a part of us. We must have the instruction of the Lord for the people He sends us to who do not know God gave us this. God calls us and trains us and He prepares the people He sends us to and accomplishes His purpose.

For years I have had this wonderful satisfaction that when God sent me He prepared me to go and He prepared the people He sent me to. It was God that brought it to pass and I know that God has accomplished His purpose. You don't have to wonder what God has accomplished inside of you.

We do not go our own way or in our own timing; but we go with the knowledge that God prepared us and the people and then He accomplishes His purpose. Otherwise when you go and preach a sermon you question it.

Did I do the right thing? Did they receive it? You don't have that kind of garbage when God prepares you. You don't have to be afraid or wonder if you did the right thing. The Spirit of the Lord is in you and He knows exactly the right people to go to. Just remember: God is putting this in us. Others fail when they are not waiting on His timing and direction. You don't fail if it is God that is doing it.

He is taking us forth to accomplish His purpose within us and we won't have it if our will is not totally submitted to Him. If we are going in His timing, it will all flow together and we don't have to be concerned about it. We don't have to have a reason for what is happening. He is fine tuning us so that we can move in the timing of the Lord. It is wonderful because you can see God's plan.

I remember when my little girl and the doctor told my husband that I couldn't get out of bed. My husband thought I was putting up an excuse for that. But the doctor said, "If you want to live to raise your children you better do what I tell you to do." By this time I had a 4th heart attack and I didn't learn to listen to the doctor the first 3 times; but I learned it by the 4th one. I was limited by what I could do. If I didn't do it somebody else would have raised my children.

So I put up with all the opposition around me and I figured nobody cared. The doctor said, "If nobody cares at least you can raise your children." We can't be foolish. If God is dealing in an area where He is disciplining us, we need to get our priorities straight!

There are times when there is a little matter of life and death. God has healed me dozens of times. One thing I know: if I hadn't obeyed the Lord and let Him do the work we wouldn't be having this meeting.

I want to encourage you not to let the enemy discourage you. I couldn't take care of David when he was born because the doctor wouldn't let me. I had to let somebody else do it. You realize that sometimes in our training someone might not understand about it. We have to be willing to let God do it. I know that we want to run with it; but we can't.

I am saying to everyone: we have to know that the Lord is speaking to us so that we can yield to His purposes. He is doing a work in us and we can't let the devil whip us. God will take us through.

Agnes I Numer with President Ronald Reagan

WE ALL HAVE A CHOICE

Jesus we thank you for your authority and your love; we thank you for your justice your mercy. Precious Lord I thank you to put into these children the training that you have for them. Lord we thank you now that the principalities have to go. These powers of hell have to go. These children have to line up according to the word of God, filled with your love and compassion. Lord, you brought them here and you're raising them here. They belong to you. We aren't going to allow a wrong spirit to rule in this place. So Lord I thank you to take dominion over the children, men and women. And Lord I thank you that this is your work and your ministry. We give glory to you and we praise you, our precious Lord Jesus. We thank you for your redemptive power and the Holy Spirit. We thank you that you are placing in us your love and an authority that comes from above.

We ask you to speak to these children. We thank you that the Spirit of the Lord is greater than the spirit of the enemy and we thank you Lord now for the outpouring of love upon these children. Everything else that is not of you Lord, I thank you to remove it. We give you glory! We praise you for the privilege of being in this place and having your presence, your love and provision. We thank you for everything that you give to us we give you glory even this night.

We thank you to bring peace to these children, with your love and give joy to them and let the other things be taken away. We give you glory for it Jesus in your wonderful name. Amen.

> Psalm 4:1 Hear me when I call, O God of my righteousness: thou hast enlarged me *when I was* in distress; have mercy upon me, and hear my prayer. 2 O ye sons of men, how long *will ye turn* my glory into shame? *how long* will ye love vanity, *and* seek after leasing? Selah. 3 But know that the LORD hath set apart him that is godly for himself: the LORD will hear when I call unto him. 4 Stand in awe, and sin not: commune with your own heart upon your bed, and be still. Selah. 5 Offer the sacrifices of righteousness, and put your trust in the LORD. 6 *There be* many that say, Who will shew us *any* good? LORD, lift thou up the light of thy countenance upon us. 7 Thou hast put gladness in my heart, more than in the time *that* their corn and their wine increased. 8 I will both lay me down in peace, and sleep: for thou, LORD, only makest me dwell in safety. Psalm 4:1-8

> Psalm 5:1 Give ear to my words, O LORD, consider my meditation. 2 Hearken unto the voice of my cry, my King, and my God: for unto thee will I pray. 3 My voice shalt thou hear in the morning, O LORD; in the morning will I direct *my prayer* unto thee, and will look up. 4 For thou *art* not a God that hath pleasure in wickedness: neither shall evil

dwell with thee. 5 The foolish shall not stand in thy sight: thou hatest all workers of iniquity. 6 Thou shalt destroy them that speak leasing: the LORD will abhor the bloody and deceitful man. 7 But as for me, I will come *into* thy house in the multitude of thy mercy: *and* in thy fear will I worship toward thy holy temple. 8 Lead me, O LORD, in thy righteousness because of mine enemies; make thy way straight before my face. 9 For *there is* no faithfulness in their mouth; their inward part *is* very wickedness; their throat *is* an open sepulchre; they flatter with their tongue. 10 Destroy thou them, O God; let them fall by their own counsels; cast them out in the multitude of their transgressions; for they have rebelled against thee. 11 But let all those that put their trust in thee rejoice: let them ever shout for joy, because thou defendest them: let them also that love thy name be joyful in thee. 12 For thou, LORD, wilt bless the righteous; with favor wilt thou compass him as *with* a shield. Psalm 5:1-12

Psalm 6:1 O LORD, rebuke me not in thine anger, neither chasten me in thy hot displeasure. 2 Have mercy upon me, O LORD; for I *am* weak: O LORD, heal me; for my bones are vexed. 3 My soul is also sore vexed: but thou, O LORD, how long? 4 Return, O LORD, deliver my soul: oh save me for thy mercies' sake. 5 For in death *there is* no remembrance of thee: in the grave who shall give thee thanks? 6 I am weary with my groaning; all the night make I my bed to swim; I water my couch with my tears. 7 Mine eye is consumed because of grief; it waxes old because of all mine enemies. 8 Depart from me, all ye workers of iniquity; for the LORD hath heard the voice of my weeping. 9 The LORD hath heard my supplication; the LORD will receive my prayer. 10 Let all mine enemies be ashamed and sore vexed: let them return *and* be ashamed suddenly. Psalm 6:1-10

Psalm 7:1 O LORD my God, in thee do I put my trust: save me from all them that persecute me, and deliver me: 2 Lest he tear my soul like a lion, rending *it* in pieces, while *there is* none to deliver. 3 O LORD my God, if I have done this; if there be iniquity in my hands; 4 If I have rewarded evil unto him that was at peace with me; (yea, I have delivered him that without cause is mine enemy:) 5 Let the enemy persecute my soul, and take *it*; yea, let him tread down my life upon the earth, and lay mine honour in the dust. Selah. 6 "Arise, O LORD, in thine anger, lift up thyself because of the rage of mine enemies: and awake for me *to* the judgment *that* thou hast commanded. 7 So shall the congregation of the people compass thee about: for their sakes therefore return thou on high. 8 The LORD shall judge the people: judge me, O LORD, according to my righteousness, and according to mine integrity *that is* in me. Psalm 7:1-8

First we call upon Him and ask Him to enlarge us and have mercy on us and hear our prayer. He's telling us what to do so that we can hear Him. It says that the Lord has set apart him that is godly for himself and the Lord will hear when we call unto Him. We often wonder if He hears our prayers; but the Lord is saying if we know He's set apart the godly for Himself then we know that He hears us when we pray. He says to stand in awe of God and don't sin: talk to Him with your own heart upon your bed, and be still. Put your trust in the Lord. Lord, you have put gladness in my heart, more than in the time of prosperity. David says He will lay me down in peace and sleep: for the Lord only makest him dwell in safety.

We have to know that the Lord is speaking to us. Our commitment to God has to come first, that we come to Him with a broken and contrite heart. We must come with an open mind and we repent and ask forgiveness. We repent for all the things that we have done. Then He hears our prayer and forgives our sins and blots them out. He wants us to know that He hears us when we call and He will answer us. In the wee hours of the night we can talk with Him on our bed.

Do you know if God is in us we aren't alone? If He's inside of us you don't have to go somewhere else to talk to Him. You don't have to go out into the field and talk to Him you can but here you have the privilege of doing it on your bed. He wants us to know Him and know that when we pray He answers us. He wants us to have that intimate relationship with us. With your own heart upon your own bed and be still the Lord talks to us in the wee hours of the morning. He might wake us up at 3 and 4 in the morning or maybe He wants to stand in the corner too. If He's in you, you don't have to go off somewhere else, you just talk to Him and He'll give you answers and He'll lead you by His Spirit.

One time a lady came to my house and she said, "The Lord sent me to take you to my house so the Lord can talk to you." That was new to me, because the Lord talked to me at the clothes line, kitchen sink, scrubbing the floors, running the vacuum and making my beds; I didn't have to go anywhere else. So the Lord said to me, "I didn't send her to tell you to go to her house. If you had gone to her house and spent the night so I could talk to you, it wouldn't have been me talking to you; because I talk to you all over the place."

God wants us to have an intimate relationship with Him. Remember He does hear our prayers. He forgives our sins and cleanses us from all unrighteousness. What a joy it is to know that we have a peace and can lay down in peace and sleep and dwell in safety. God has called us to a life of peace and rest, not many people in the world have this. We have to give our life to the Lord in total commitment to Him. He's not going to meet our needs half way and we can't come half way to Him we have to come all the way. He requires of us total surrender to Him. Let me tell you it is kind of one sided, I think. What's He taking away from us? Sin and darkness, evil habits and alcohol, drugs and all the lust of the flesh and the pride of life! He's taking it all away and you are free. Why do you look back and let the devil torment your mind instead of thinking: I'm free, I'm free! The Lord has set me free!

God has a way for you and that is the way of His peace, His righteousness, His forgiveness and healing. We can't play with Him or the devil. But God says stand in awe and sin not and commune with your own heart upon your bed and be still. Peace comes from God, joy comes from God, salvation comes from Him and love comes from Him. The Lord is calling us into His love; into this very beautiful relationship He's talking about here in Psalm 4. God's presence can be in us. God wants us to put our trust in Him instead of trusting in our flesh. I want you to know you are a chosen people and He's chosen you to be 100% in Him so that He can train you so He can be 100% in you out there against the evil of this world. God is saying that He hears our cries. He not only hears our cry but answers it; because He has called us to a different walk in this life. He wants to show you who He is! You can go on with your business and do your own thing, but then you will never know what God will do for you. You will never know unless you put your trust in Him and let Him show you that He is God.

We can be our own God but we aren't going very far if we are. We can do our own thing and He won't stop you because He honors your right to choose. One thing the Lord taught me some 40 years ago is that I have no right to interfere with the choice that anyone is making. I have to stand back and let them make it, because they have the right to make it whether it is right or wrong. Unless the Holy Ghost says to me I'm drawing the plum line and this is the last time I'm coming this way. When He says that I have to obey Him and He has done it. There was a family here from Porto Rica. He had a wife and two children and they came to us for help in the middle of the night. The man came for deliverance. He had principalities and powers that were very evil. So we prayed and fasted for Him and the Lord delivered him. His wife wasn't too concerned about God except when she needed Him then she would think of Him. So one day the Lord sent some of us to their house. I want you to read

> The LORD repented for this: This also shall not be, saith the Lord GOD. 7 Thus he shewed me: and, behold, the Lord stood upon a wall *made* by a plumbline, with a plumbline in his hand. 8 And the LORD said unto me, Amos, what seest thou? And I said, A plumbline. Then said the Lord, Behold, I will set a plumbline in the midst of my people Israel: I will not again pass by them any more: Amos 7:6-8

The Lord told me I want you to go to that home and I want you to read this scripture to them. I went that night with David and someone else and the Lord gave them the word.

My son said to the wife: "Do you know something about the Lord." She said, "I think of the Lord when I need Him." I thought this was awfully strange that she had no communication with God at all.

That night after we left the husband walked out of that house never to return again. Sometime later he was in a motorcycle accident and was taken to intensive care in the hospital where I went to see him. He had divorced his wife and gone his own way and married someone else. I went into the intensive care to talk to him. I believe he had made his peace with God and was a Christian, he passed away. She wasn't going the way God wanted her to, because she had no interest in Him except when she needed Him. Five years later this little boy who had been so much like his dad he carried a Bible around and said, "I'm going to be a preacher." We were called to the mortuary and by this time the lad was 16 years old. He had joined devil worshipers and all of his friends were devil worshipers. We walked into that mortuary and I was so thankful she never asked me to do that funeral. She called me in the middle of the night and said this young man about 3 in the morning was crossing the street and a car ran him down and killed him instantly. She calls me to tell me about it.

When we went to the mortuary his friends were very sad. We said, "Didn't you know that Arthur didn't make it to God? He made a choice and joined the gangs and lost his life without God." They said, "Not our friend Arthur this couldn't happen to him." We said, "Do you know Arthur is in hell now?" "Not our friend Arthur!" "Yes! Your friend Arthur because he chose the evil rather than the good!"

I prayed for some of these people that were all dressed in black. They didn't look like human beings. It was so terrible. I thought of this little boy carrying a Bible around. This is why we have to watch over the children. This is why we are responsible to bring them in the ways of the Lord and to have God in your life.

When we choose our own way and God has called us to His way there is trouble. Little did I know that night that God had put the plum line down and He wasn't going that way again. Little did I know what was going to happen to that entire family!

We have the Lord. We have choices to make with our whole heart and our whole life. But if we want our own way God will not stop you from it; but your own way will take you away from God. We need Him take out of us everything that is contrary to His perfect will and to put His love in us until ever thing is filled with His love. It's up to us to choose it, because God made us free. He won't interfere; but we have a choice to make.

I was in Africa with Geri and we were in a village having a meeting. We went into this village and a man rushes in there to hear. There were several men out there and a man came in and said, "I have to talk to you!" He told us this story: He said He was a business man and God was blessing Him; but He became greedy. He wasn't satisfied with the blessings of the Lord. He started some deals with people and the Lord told him it was bribery. He didn't think it was bribery, he thought it was his friends. One day he said, "God, I don't want anything more to do with you; I'm done with you. Devil I'll let you come you come and live in me." God said, "Wait a minute I'm not finished with you." He wasn't going to get off the hook that easy. So the man told us his story and I didn't think any more about it.

We went into another city where I had a friend I haven't seen in years. He came to me in his car and said, "Agnes I want to take you to this hospital to meet this doctor. So he drove me to this hospital and the name of this hospital was "By His Stripes."

As I walked in there and he gave me a little booklet and it told the story of this man that we had seen in the village. He said, "One morning a man came in and we prayed for him and the Lord healed him." This man said, "God I'm finished with you, I'm going to go with Satan." God said, "No, I'm not finished with you." This was Monday when the Lord told him to get his house in order. "You get everything straight and ask everyone to forgive you. You ask God to forgive you." So he remembered this one woman that he had a lot of hate against her. He goes to see her and asked her to forgive him; but she threw hot soup in his face.

He wondered what he was going to do. Eventually she got to him and he forgave her. He only had one week to save his life. The Lord said to him on Monday "Saturday you are going to die. Get your house in order." This time he wasn't fooling around and he knew it was the Lord. On Saturday he was healthy there was nothing wrong with him, but he died. His family brought him to this hospital dead. He was a corpse and there was nothing they could do. Sunday morning they brought this body into the hospital and were told that they didn't have time for that, they couldn't handle a corpse.

He had his Sunday school class and he was going to his class they had the story of Lazarus. As he was hearing this story of

Lazarus the Lord said, "You take this corpse and bring him to your hospital." His head nurse said, "This man's dead. It's a corpse." The doctor said, "Put an I.V. in him." The nurse said, "He doesn't have any veins." The Doctor said, ""Put it where you know the veins are." He was dead for four days. The Doctor put him in the bed and the head nurse had trouble with him. The doctor went home and thought he would rest for a little while for he felt very tired. The Lord took him by the spirit to follow this man. The man went into the heavens. I don't want to give you details of it because I'm going to read it you. It is awesome what God did.

When he got in there God said, "I've got 4 counts against you. He had done everything the Lord had told him to do, but he wasn't sure the Lord had forgiven him. He gets there and here's this big book. They opened it up to see if his name was written in the book of life and there were four counts against you.

So they came with a bottle and a brush; in that bottle was the blood of Jesus. He stood there and didn't know what was going to happen because he wasn't sure the Lord was going to clear his record. They took that brush and washed away the 4 charges against him. The Lord did it in front of him. He sees a friend behind him who was a Christian and he hears them say to him "Depart from me I never knew you." Others came and He said, "Depart from me I never knew you." They went through the procedures that were necessary and when he got to a certain point and the Lord told him, "You have to go back."

The doctor heard what the Lord was saying to this man. The Lord took the doctor back to his bedroom. So as he was waiting for this man to wake up. Everyday he thought he would go and the man would come back from heaven. He was sure he would find this man awake and he would be alright. But it wasn't, so 4 days went by and on the 4th day there was on tears coming from his eye. That was the first sign of life. And the Lord restored him for one purpose: "You go and tell my people there's no purgatory! There's heaven and hell. You choose one or the other to go to and go warn my people."

The choice we make depends on where we are going to live for eternity. This doctor gave me the little book. I loaned it to someone that was praying and I never got it back; but I have another copy. I have a story of this man's life and I know he's still living and still giving God the glory and telling the people there's no purgatory; there's only one way: that's through Jesus.

There's no other way that we are going to come to God but through Jesus.

We have to guard our ways and know that we are going to do what God wants us to do and make sure that we obey him. There's no room for game playing; there's only two places to go.

When I was 16, I'd gone so far down away from God that the Lord shook me over hell. He opened it up and he said to me if you don't serve me that is where you will go. That's as straight as it is. If we don't serve him, that's where we're going to go. It's no games.

Think of what God is going to give to us in exchange. How can we resist His love, and that all He has given us. Do we prefer all this stuff in our life? He can send us to hell if that is what we choose; or are we willing to let him clean our house and fill us with His love until our being is saturated with the love of God.

I'm not a hell fire preacher, but I know very well what hell is like. I know the price that we have to pay if we don't walk with God with all our heart. The people who don't want to help the poor, one day before very long, they are going to stand before God. And God's not going to ask them how many thousands of souls they have brought into the kingdom. There's one question he's going to ask: I was hungry and you fed me not, I was thirsty and you gave me no drink. I was a stranger and you took me not in, I was naked and you clothed me not. I was sick and you visited me not, I was in prison and you didn't come.

I don't care how big we are. If we're not doing the command of the Lord, we're going to miss it. Isaiah 58 is very loud and clear and God requires it of us. Maybe you don't want to do it, but if you love God it's in your heart to meet their needs. There's only one outlet on this earth to God's love and His kingdom. That's in brotherly kindness; loving one another, serving one another, helping the poor and meeting the needs that Jesus laid before us in the gospels. That which Jesus did He requires of us to do.

I thank God for all of you who have vision, you have His love and you have His desire to fulfill His promises to others. We have a straight line and I don't mind walking that line, because it's a line of peace, joy, righteousness and holiness with the Lord. We need the understanding. God's calling a people that He can love and sing to and he can rejoice over as we walk and run in His love to the nations of the world.

It is very awesome what God has in store for us as we empty out everything and let His love fill us. The one thing that was missing with that woman that was sent to hell: she didn't have God's love. That was the only thing that they had to say against her. If the love of the world is in us, the love of the Father isn't. If we love the Father the love of the world isn't in us. But God is drawing a straight line in our lives so He can fill us with His love and His love can flow through us.

He'll make the way for us; we don't have to make it our self. If we make it our self we are going to miss it. If we give it to him He will direct it. We are going to have that peace and joy and righteousness.

The Lord wouldn't let me stop talking to the people who came today even though I could see where it was going. The bride to be and his mother heard it all and they received it. God had a purpose for it. Maybe the Lord will be able to break through the barriers with him and show him the proof. It's better to have Jesus in charge of our life with His love and glory and kingdom operating in us. We have a choice to make. If we choose him we shall eternally be blessed by Him and live in His kingdom for ever. If we don't choose Him we will be damned forever.

It's not a little thing: we need to choose Him. He loves us He doesn't want us to go to the place the devil is going. He wants us to go to the place that He has chosen for us. He won't force or compel us except by His love to draw us unto him. We have His love that is compelling us to follow Him.

I want to leave these words with you, choose Him, there isn't anything lacking in what He wants for us if we will but follow Him. God has given us so much that if we will hear what He's saying we don't have to entangle ourselves with other things. It's so clear and simple and mighty if we receive it and be willing to walk that path of liberty, peace, joy, righteousness and holiness. We can impart it to you if you want it. That's the responsibility that God has given to me and you. He will impart it to you. So great is this word if we hear and receive it.

Father, we thank you for this word. Jesus we thank you, you don't say one thing and do another. You don't want us saying one thing and doing something else. Lord, speak to our hearts and let us know your great love and provision that you have made for us that you might take this gospel of the Kingdom of Jesus Christ into all the world and that we might be a witness to all nations so you can return again to your people.

Lord Jesus, speak your love and comfort to us with your strength. Lord, the blessings with your bountiful provision that you have given to us wen receive with a grateful and thankful heart. We thank everyone that's had a part in bringing it to pass. Lord, let your Spirit flow through us and move in our lives so that we choose to walk in the spirit of life. Lord Jesus, now bring life to everyone that is here; your life that we may live throughout all eternity. We rejoice in everything that you have done for us for you said you will not hold anyone guiltless who turned away from Christ or rejected Him. Lord we thank you for the truth and the truth will make us free. Jesus, I thank you for ears to hear and a heart to receive. Amen.

WHAT DOES HE REQUIRE OF US?

Turn to Psalm 2, it asks a question.

> Psalm 2:1 Why do the heathen rage, and the people imagine a vain thing? 2 The kings of the earth set themselves, and the rulers take counsel together, against the LORD, and against his anointed, *saying*, 3 Let us break their bands asunder, and cast away their cords from us. 4 He that sitteth in the heavens shall laugh: the Lord shall have them in derision. 5 Then shall he speak unto them in his wrath, and vex them in his sore displeasure. 6 Yet have I set my king upon my holy hill of Zion. 7 I will declare the decree: the LORD hath said unto me, Thou *art* my Son; this day have I begotten thee. 8 Ask of me, and I shall give *thee* the heathen *for* thine inheritance, and the uttermost parts of the earth *for* thy possession. 9 Thou shalt break them with a rod of iron; thou shalt dash them in pieces like a potter's vessel. 10 Be wise now therefore, O ye kings: be instructed, ye judges of the earth. 11 Serve the LORD with fear, and rejoice with

trembling. 12 Kiss the Son, lest he be angry, and ye perish *from* the way, when his wrath is kindled but a little. Blessed *are* all they that put their trust in him. Psalm 2:1-12

The Lord created man to love Him; but He also gave us a free will. I feel that God is saying, "Now I am going to show this world that I am God." He can't go into these countries that have said, "You can't come in." Places with Hinduism, Buddhism, Muslims and everything else have closed their borders to Christianity. They said, "You're not welcome God, you can't come in." I want to read another scripture to you, Psalm 24.

Can you think for a moment what it would be like to be the creator of the universe and be denied by the people that you created and are saying that you don't even exist? Can you think of that?

> Psalm 24:1 The earth *is* the LORD'S, and the fullness thereof; the world, and they that dwell therein. 2 For he hath founded it upon the seas, and established it upon the floods. 3 Who shall ascend into the hill of the LORD? or who shall stand in his holy place? 4 He that hath clean hands, and a pure heart; who hath not lifted up his soul unto vanity, nor sworn deceitfully. 5 He shall receive the blessing from the LORD, and righteousness from the God of his salvation. 6. This *is* the generation of them that seek him, that seek thy face, O Jacob. Selah. 7 Lift up your heads, O ye gates; and be ye lift up, ye everlasting doors; and the King of glory shall come in. 8 Who *is* this King of glory? The LORD strong and mighty, the LORD mighty in battle. 9 Lift up your heads, O ye gates; even lift *them* up, ye

everlasting doors; and the King of glory shall come in. 10 Who is this King of glory? The LORD of hosts, he *is* the King of glory. Selah. Psalm 24:1-10

What is He saying? "This King of glory!" Why is He stressing in Psalm 2 and Psalm 24 the King of glory? Because His King of glory is in Zion! Where are we? We're supposed to be in Zion aren't we? Who is in charge of us? The King of glory!

Turn to Isaiah 59. The situation that He's talking about in this chapter is where judgment is turned away backward, and justice stands afar off, truth is fallen in the street, and equity can't enter. Truth failed and He that departs from you shall make himself a smear. The Lord saw it and it displeased Him that there was no judgment and He saw that there was no man and wondered that there was no intercessor; therefore His arm brought salvation unto him and His righteousness sustained him.

> Isaiah 59:17 For he put on righteousness as a breastplate, and an helmet of salvation upon his head; and he put on the garments of vengeance *for* clothing, and was clad with zeal as a cloke. 18 According to *their* deeds, accordingly he will repay, fury to his adversaries, recompence to his enemies; to the islands he will repay recompence. 19 So shall they fear the name of the LORD from the west, and his glory from the rising of the sun. When the enemy shall come in like a flood, the Spirit of the LORD shall lift up a standard against him. 20 And the Redeemer shall come to Zion, and unto them that turn from transgression in Jacob, saith the LORD. 21 As for me, this *is* my covenant with them, saith the LORD; My spirit that *is* upon thee, and my words which

I have put in thy mouth, shall not depart out of thy mouth, nor out of the mouth of thy seed, nor out of the mouth of thy seed's seed, saith the LORD, from henceforth and for ever. Is. 59:17-21

Yet have I set my king upon my holy hill of Zion. 7 I will declare the decree: the LORD hath said unto me, Thou *art* my Son; this day have I begotten thee. 8 Ask of me, and I shall give *thee* the heathen *for* thine inheritance, and the uttermost parts of the earth *for* thy possession. Psalm 2:6-8

Why was this declaration made at this particular time? Because the leaders of nations said, "We're not going to allow God or His anointed ones to come into our nations." Years ago I asked the Lord a question. I said, "Lord why don't you show this world who you are? They curse you, they revile you and they don't want to believe in you; they mock you just like it says here in Psalm 2."

He gave me a scripture, and He gave me an answer. He said,

> And delivered his strength into captivity, and his glory into the enemy's hand. Psalm 78:61

I believe that He's now taking it out of the enemies' hands and He's going to take over.

> Then the Lord awaked as one out of sleep, *and* like a mighty man that shouteth by reason of wine. 66 And he smote his enemies in the hinder parts: he put them to a perpetual reproach. Psalm 78:65-66

Why? They declared, "God's not coming into our country." The Communists rose up and the Communists said, "The world is going into Communism and there's no God." The Chinese went into Communism and they had all of their God's and their idols. Then here comes the Buddhists and they have taken the world. And the Muslims declare that they're taking over America and they're doing a good job of it. Why? Because the Christians are asleep!

"I'm going to show this world I am God." When He told me this, when I was a teenager, I knew the day would come and He would give me the privilege of knowing when He was going to take over.

When I was in Colorado Springs in 1998 He declared that He had raised His scepter and He said, "Now I am going to take over." It was very mighty, very emphatic. I don't know what anybody else felt; but I knew one thing, God had risen up and said now I'm going to show the world that I created it and everybody in it, and I'm going into those nations and I'm going to show them my love and my glory.

He is sending His judgment over every nation. Where are we supposed to be while He is doing this? I believe God reunited the business world where they should have been all the time; but man had separated them the way they pleased. The church became so holy that they had no time to feed the hungry or clothe the naked or do anything but be holy. It displeased God. He had an appointed time and that time is now. The body of Christ has to come back into line with what God has ordained it to be; not what we think it should be. I've had many churches say to me, "It's the job of the welfare, to feed the hungry. It's not our job." They're going to stand before Him one day and what a shock they're going to have. He said, "I was hungry and you didn't feed me. Depart from me you workers of inequity." How are we going to handle it if we neglect to do what God's called us to do? We get caught up in our stinking flesh and we don't pay attention to what God is saying to us. We need to shake ourselves and realize that we have a responsibility before almighty God to take this gospel of Jesus Christ to the nations.

We play our games; we can't even do our jobs. When somebody tells us the right way to do it we get into an argument. Where are we today? Where is our heart and why are we bickering? Why are we complaining while the world goes to hell?

He said, "I have set my king on Zion, my holy hill. I will declare the degree." You're not at Sommer Haven just to be at Sommer Haven. You're not here to do your own will or walk your own way. There are teachers and you need to hear what they say and do it the way they say it, even if you don't like it. It will change your lives!

When Jesus went back to be with the Father, what did he say? I want to read a verse.

> As thou hast sent me into the world, even so have I also sent them into the world. John 17:18

This is the commission that God gave to us! He goes back to His Father, what is His command? Take this gospel of the kingdom to the ends of the earth. What have we done with it? We've got everything but the kingdom: we're demonstrating our doctrines, demonstrating the way we want to live.

What about the way of the kingdom? We have a King and He's on His Holy hill. What is He doing? What are we allowing Him to do? He prayed Father, I would that they go with me to heaven. I'm going to shock you; He didn't save you just to go to heaven. He saved us to go to the world and then the reward of it is heaven. The job of it is on the earth, heaven doesn't need it, the world needs it. Jesus prayed the Father, I will that they also, whom thou hast given me, be with me where I am; that they may behold my glory, which thou hast given me: for thou lovest me before the foundation of the world. O righteous Father, the world hath not known thee: but I have known thee, and these have known that thou hast sent me; but Jesus said, I must send them to the world.

Our doctrine has been all messed up because all we think about is getting saved and going to heaven. The truth is, that inside of us, is the kingdom of God and our reward is heaven. The King of glory should live in you and you should be taking instructions from Him; not you telling Him what to do.

> As thou hast sent me into the world, even so have I also sent them into the world. John 17:18

It doesn't matter what the world thinks and we already know what the devil thinks. We, as Christians, can just be happy Christians; the devil isn't worried about you. But, when you obey God that is when the devil gets concerned. It's up to you, whether you're going to obey God or not. God has opened up the nations to us, but we can't do it alone. We have to allow God to train us. Some awesome things are happening, some awesome things happened on the face of this earth. He's bringing judgment to the nations, but He's also bringing judgment to us as we strip ourselves from our stinking flesh and let the King of glory take His place inside of us. We're hindering the process of the Lord as long as we dwell in our flesh. Get rid of it and let God use you. I'm sure the King of glory, in you, is not going to comfort your flesh. He's going to clean it out, so His love can come in you and then you can take it to the nations. You're not going without Him, He only has us to do it.

What are we doing about it? We heard there's a mighty cyclone in Africa and India. Now India is a little harder nut to crack because it's all Hindu and it doesn't want God; but nothing is going to stop God from taking over India.

What part do we have in it? On Friday of next week there's a convention going on in India. It's a business meeting of the leaders of nations. We need to pray. When this cyclone hit Orica, India God declared, "I am God. I'm taking over India," and He's doing it. I felt in my spirit it can't be a little thing; it has to be an explosive thing to jar India with God's light. Please pray for Bro. Shaker because He will be here tomorrow but only for a few days. The day He arrives back in India he is going before the leaders of nations that are coming to India and God is going to use Him to speak to them concerning what God's going to do. The Lord gave me a word to focus in on India. We are focusing in on India right now, because God is going to bring His love, His light and His glory to India. 330 million gods are not any challenge to God.

On my first trip into India a very strange thing happened to me. I was going with a Charismatic Catholic group. I went two weeks ahead of them and I had just met Bro. Joseph in Hubly and he had asked me to come to see him. I went to see him two weeks ahead of the group and he met me in Bombay; for Hubly is 100 miles from the airport in Bombay.

He said, "Agnes I want to show you Bombay." It happened to be the biggest festivity of lights by the Hindu religion. What do they do on that day? They have carts and trucks and haul their idols down the middle of their streets. On each side of the street there are millions of people bowing down to these idols. We get caught in the middle of the travel and we're not going anywhere very fast. The Lord said to me, "I want you to pray in the spirit that I will bind the powers of the idols on the minds of the people." Now here they are bowing down on both sides of the street to these idols. I am in the middle of the traffic riding right along with them. I had another reason for being there; for the Spirit of the Lord was binding the powers that be, off the minds of these people as they were going down the street. I didn't know when I was going to India this was going to happen to me. I didn't know how God was going to use me; but He did.

We were in Hubli with all this land, nothing but land. He was just starting this ministry, so we prayed over all the land, that God would give it to him for the ministry; for him to do what he was called to do. One man named Bro. Joseph had died in an accident, his wife Rosie and the wife of their son Leslie died also. She and Leslie were only married 20 days when the accident happened. The Lord told me in 1997, "I want you to go back to India." I went back to Leslie's wedding. There I saw two orphanages on the land that we had prayed for. I saw a bible school and a clinic and a church; all the product of God's spirit.

I came into Bombay on my first trip and I've never been with Catholics in my life. I didn't know anything about Pentecost, because I was a Nazarene, but God started enlightening me by experience for my friends were all Catholic. Something happened to me at that convention; I found myself with the priest and the nuns. They were taking me everywhere. The last day of that convention they said, "Will you be the speaker?" I wasn't Catholic; I didn't know anything about it. There were six groups in Bombay alone and they would all gather in one meeting and they asked me to be the speaker. I had no idea when I went to India what was going to happen.

In 1998 this woman who doesn't know me or anything about me said that what God did was small compared to what God was going to do now. God sent me to Rome and I met the Pope. I prayed over thousands to know Jesus. What is it? God's heart is to draw the whole world to Him that everyone would know Him. We have to allow the Spirit of the Lord to direct us. One day the Lord said to me, "If you ask me I'll give them to you." I said, "Lord I ask you for the heathen for my inheritance and the outermost parts of the earth for my possession." That was a pretty big blessing wasn't it? He told me to ask. He said, "I'll give them to you. Then He said, "Call upon me and I will answer. I will do a great and mighty thing." I said, "Lord, I will call upon you." Both of those things have been very prevalent in my life; because I asked and He answered. He said to me at that time, "If I don't have it, I'll create it for you." I believe it! Yesterday I had an experience and I very quickly realized God was fulfilling that promise. If we don't have it, He'll create it for us.

Where are we in the promise? What does He require of us? How do we stand with Him in comparison to that which He requires of us? Where are we in the kingdom? Jesus said Go ye into all the world and be a witness for me. Where do we stand before Him? What does He require of us? I'm giving you my experience. You have your own and what are you doing with it. Are your ears tuned to Him so He can train you?

I've never believed that God established Sommer Haven for people to do their own thing. I believe that He established it so that we would flow together, in the purpose of God, that He could accomplish His purpose with us. Many people have come and gone out to do their own thing. I am not God, but I know He didn't establish us for people to walk in their own ways. He established us to walk in His ways with Him as the King of glory, clothed with vengeance against the enemy. I have one more scripture I want to read to you. I'm trying to encourage you that the King of glory wants to be King of your life.

> For every battle of the warrior *is* with confused noise, and garments rolled in blood; but *this* shall be with burning *and* fuel of fire. 6 For unto us a child is born, unto us a son is given: and the government shall be upon his shoulder: and his name shall be called Wonderful, Counsellor, The mighty God, The everlasting Father, The Prince of Peace. 7 Of the increase of *his* government and peace *there shall be* no end, upon the throne of David, and upon is kingdom, to order it, and to establish it with judgment and with justice from henceforth even for ever. Isaiah 9:5-7

Where are we today? Upon the throne of David, and upon his kingdom, to order it, and to establish it with judgment and with justice from henceforth even for ever. The zeal of the LORD of hosts will perform this."

Who is going to perform it? Jesus is clothed with vengeance! The zeal is a cloak over Him. The zeal of the Lord of hosts will perform this. Why are we complaining? Why are we afraid of the devil? The King of glory says, "Let me come in. I'll fight your battles for you. I'm all ready for it." The Lord of

Hosts shall do this. We are in another world, we are commissioned by the King of Glory.

> I will declare the decree: the LORD hath said unto me,
> Thou *art* my Son; this day have I begotten thee. Psalm 2:7

This day He wants to be King in us. He wants to have charge of His kingdom that He's placed in us, not with us ruling it; but with Him ruling it. I think it's very clear. I don't know how anyone can misunderstand it. We aren't going anywhere without Him; He has to become the King in us. I think a lot of us, when we don't want to do things, we don't do them. We have to stand before Him! Things are happening very mightily now for the Lord has arisen to show the nation that He created the earth and He created everyone in it. He's going everywhere to declare it and He's going in by judgment. These things that are going over the earth right now, I've never known before in the same measure that they are now. Our safe haven is in Christ and Christ in us. I think we need to make less decisions with our minds and let the Lord decide what He wants for us, so that we can be that vessel to obey Him.

We're going to Singapore in a few days. There we are meeting with Pastor Lawrence who has a church of 10,000. He's asked us if we will join with them in the taking of this gospel of the kingdom, to all the earth. We have meetings with different committees and the sadness of my heart is that I don't have teams here ready to go in there to teach and to train. I believe God is going to raise them up in Singapore. Many of them are Chinese. I believe He is going to raise them up there and send them out. We have much to do here; we need to become more in one accord so the Lord can minister the needs to us that we might be ready to move when He wants us to move.

Agnes I. Numer older years

Agnes I. Numer older years in her home with those that lived with her in the ministry.

THE VISION NO LONGER TARRIES

And ye shall tread down the wicked; for they shall be ashes under the souls of your feet in the day that I shall do this, saith the Lord of hosts. Malachi 4:3

Then did I beat them as small as the dust of the earth, I did stamp them as the mire of the street, *and* did spread them abroad. 2 Samuel 22:43

But unto you that fear my name… Malachi 4:2

Who are we serving? The Lord! What are we doing when we are serving the Lord? We are doing whatever He wants us to do, aren't we? It shows a whole new light on it, doesn't it?

They that wait upon the Lord shall renew their strength they shall mount up with wings as eagles … Isaiah 40:33

… the Sun of righteousness shall arise with healing in his wings; and ye shall go forth, and grow up as calves of the stall. Malachi 4:2

What are we going to do? We are going to grow up fast. If we are babes, we are going to grow up fast. We are not growing up and maturing as nature normally does; we are going to mature faster.

> But wait upon the Lord. Isaiah 40:31

We're not doing our thing, and we're not saying our own words. We are waiting upon Him and we are doing what He would have us to do.

You might ask: What do we do when we serve the Lord? Whatever He wants us to do, not what we want to do; but what He asks us to do.

> … they shall mount up with wings as eagles; they shall run, and not be weary; and they shall walk, and not faint. Isaiah 40:31

> and ye shall go forth, and grow up as calves of the stall. Malachi 4:2

These are all action, there's no hesitancy. He said,

> For the vision is yet for an appointed time, … though it tarry, wait for it; Habakkuk 2:3

If the vision no longer tarries we have to run with it. They that run, put it on tablets, and read it as they run. So we are in a hurry now and we don't have any time to waste. We are going to read it as we go. We are going to *mount up with wings as eagles* and we're not going to wait. We are going to be doing what God has called us to do as the vision comes forth. It no longer tarries; it is here, so it shall speak;

… but at the end it shall speak, and not lie: … Habakkuk 2:3

It so it shall go forth even as God has spoken it. The vision is here; the vision that God has called us to do, in him, is here and the world is in great need of it. The scriptures there in Samuel and Malachi are very appropriate scriptures because the Lord is speaking to a particular people that put their trust in the Lord. A lot of people say they put their trust in the Lord, but the test comes when the trials come. And then we find out whether our trust is in the Lord, these remain …

One thing we fail to have as we should is the fear of God. God is calling us to really let him put in us the reverence of God that we will know.

> … the Sun of righteousness shall arise with healing in his wings; and ye shall go forth, and grow up as calves of the stall. Malachi 4:2

> … they shall mount up with wings as eagles; Is 40:31

You waiting is going to be what God wants you to do, trusting him and believing that what He wants will certainly come to pass. These things which He has spoken are coming to pass very rapidly, all over the world. There are stories everywhere about the mighty works of God, there are strange things happening. Different ones are talking about what God does and we are seeing the strange things God is doing. Some things He has never done before, He is doing now! Different ways that man is baffled or puzzled; it is hard to realize that God would do the things He does today. But God is doing things, today, He never did before and His word says that. He is going to be glorified. For only the Lord will be able to accomplish these things for us, He is going to call us a people that know the Living God.

We are thinking about China and some of the other countries that don't know of the greatness of our God. God is going to do strange things there, so that they might know that it isn't one of their gods, but it is the Living God that is doing it. God is saying we have a work to do; mainly that His love and His spirit flow through us that others will see Jesus in us. Let us handle things the way the Lord wants us to do them.

What we would reason out ourselves will not be the way the Lord would want you to do it! He has his own way of doing things. He says,

> ... the Sun of righteousness shall arise with healing in his wings; and ye shall go forth, and grow up as calves of the stall. Malachi 4:2

> ... and ye shall go forth, and grow up as calves of the stall. Malachi 4:2

We have been seeing a lot of growing up the last few days seeing these young men sprout up quickly, like in one day. We are seeing it and we are giving God glory for it. All at once they are springing forth and getting ready to run and not being weary and not be fainting. Then He says,

> And ye shall tread down the wicked; for they shall be ashes under the soles of your feet ... Malachi 4:3

It doesn't say as ashes, but ashes under your feet. The wicked are going to be powder; just as He says in Samuel. They are going to be powder; they are going to be dust. For God is defeating the enemy and all of his plans and purposes. He says our enemies will be under our feet.

We praise him tonight and give him glory because He is going to cause us to arise; He will arise in us that we might go forth. You know when you go to a meeting like this something happens to you. You are ready to run; ready to do what God wants you to do. God is preparing us! I have a strong awareness of what the Lord is doing it and it's not us; it's His Spirit.

> And ye shall tread down the wicked; for they shall be ashes under the soles of your feet in the day that I shall do *this*, saith the LORD of hosts. Malachi 4:3

That doesn't mean maybe, it means He absolutely shall do it.

So why does He cause this thing to come in this hour? Why is He causing the healing to come forth?

> … the Sun of righteousness shall arise with healing in his wings; … Malachi 4:2

What are we going to do? What has God purposed for us? There is a healing of the nations coming. Right now the whole world needs it so desperately; but something has to happen to the Christians. Something has to happen to the body of Christ.

How many in the world today would come to the Lord? Something has to happen! The fear of the Lord has to come in His people, the Sun of righteousness has to arise inside us. We need the fear of God not the fear of man! We need the awesome fear of His presence to hear what He wants us to do. We must have this healing; something is going to happen to us. We won't be able to stand still, just like we are now. We won't keep our feet still because the spirit of dancing will be here. We aren't going to be able to keep from running if He lets us out. Just like calves of the stall, you, and all of us, are going to run and jump and hop in every direction.

Have you ever taken a calf out of a stall? You try to catch one of them and you can't. The Lord is letting us out to run and not be weary, to walk and not faint; because He has a purpose for this hour: that His 'church arise'. As they arise He will lift them up and cause them to have the fear of God in them. Only then can we do His will and we can be a servant and move as a servant to him, wherever He sends us. Whatever He says for us to do we will do and whatever He tells us to say we will say. A lot of preparation is needed and the realization that we must know him.

Many years ago I had an anticipation of what was going to happen when the Lord started moving. I waited with eagerness for I could feel what God was going to do in this day. I now realize this is the time in history when the Sun of righteous is arising with healing in His wings and we shall go forth and grow up as calves of the stall and put the wicked under our feet.

> *Let* the high *praises* of God *be* in their mouth and a two-edged sword in their hand; 7 To execute vengeance upon the heathen, *and* punishments upon the people; Psalm 149:6-7

That's what we are going to do. There's a spirit of burning and the spirit of judgment against the powers and works of Satan. The spirit of burning is to burn up the spirit of the flesh. He is going to do a complete job with us against the devil's territory. He said, "I have come to Judge Satan and everything that belongs to him." God will judge it and remove it. He will burn anything of the flesh; hay, wood, and stubble, there will be nothing left.

We aren't anybody, but we are saying, "Lord, let the Sun of righteousness arise with healing in His wings." First must come and awesome awareness of His presence. We must be aware that the Lord is doing something and we are a part of His plan to take this gospel of the kingdom to the nations of the world. You aren't going to take it in your flesh, you will take it with the Sun of righteousness in you; that will cause you to grow up as calves of the stall; to run and not be weary; but to mount up with wings as eagles. We have to take it and run with it, for it is time now to run. It is to be manifested and demonstrated by the Spirit of God.

> Whereby are given unto us exceeding great and precious promises: that by these ye might be partakers of the divine nature, having escaped the corruption that is in the world through lust. 2 Pe 1:4

Peter speaks concerning God's love through which we are partakers of His divine nature. These things which God has given to us will not make us half way what He wants us to be. They will make us, all the way, what He wants us to be. And add to your faith virtue; and to virtue knowledge. We have His righteousness and His knowledge abiding in us that Christ is revealed to us; which righteousness is not our own. It is His faith working in us; it is His knowledge working in us along with His virtue. He doing it all in earthen vessels! He is going to cause it to be carried to the nations. He is building something in us and the final part of that building is His love and that love is going to change our lives and the lives of those around us.

There's only one way that we can change other lives: through brotherly kindness! How are we demonstrating brotherly kindness here? If you look at it here, this is all about the promises; all this here is about what God is doing changing us. Down through the years I wondered why brotherly kindness is stuck in there; I couldn't see where it fit in. One day the Lord opened it up to me and I realized that love couldn't be demonstrated anywhere, except through brotherly kindness. There's only one outlet and that's brotherly kindness.

What does it mean? It means a lot of things; that is the full answer. Isn't that mighty? This is what He is talking about? It is not for us; but to give to meet the needs of others. God is calling His church to repent because we have neglected to meet the needs of others. That's what you have been called to do.

They tell me all of the time, "But I'm not called to do that." If you see a brother in need and you don't help him, it doesn't have my name on it, it has all of our names on it. We have to realize it; we have to take heed to it. The fruit of it is astonishing; the fruit of it is the changing of lives. It isn't just what we are doing; but what He has persuaded us to do that others might know that He loved them and died for them. We give it to them as to the Lord. It is hay, wood and stubble and it will burn up if it is not full of God's love. He has called us to do these things and we will stand before Him.

We will do that which He has called us to do and boldly in that day. Not any boldness of our flesh, but He has done it and we can give him the glory. There is also a scripture there. He is talking about how we tell the true from the false. I think this is going to be more and more pronounced in our life. The word says,

> Ye are of God, little children, and have overcome them: because greater is he that is in you, than he that is in the world. 5 They are of the world: therefore speak they of the world, and the world heareth them. 6 We are of God: he that knoweth God heareth us; he that is not of God heareth not us. Hereby know we the spirit of truth, and the spirit of error. 1 John 4:4-6

Let's see what it means, have you ever been with people where your speech bares witness with God? And you have been with other Christian people and you don't feel the speech bares witness? Have you been with people that thought you weren't of God? The test is we are of God if we know that God dwells in us, and we are around other people that are called Christians, but they don't believe it.

What is your test here? If they hear us they are of God, if they don't hear us they are not. That's pretty strong isn't it? If they hear you they are of God; therefore you know the spirit of truth and the spirit of error. Smoother and smoother comes the work of Satan, he comes in like an angel of light. It is going to get slick because of the deception, because of the anti-Christ movement comes a great falseness, it is so cleverly done.

> For there shall arise false Christs, and false prophets, and shall shew great signs and wonders; insomuch that, if it

were possible, they shall deceive the very elect. Matthew 24:24

The Bible says if it were possible the very elect would be deceived; but Jesus prayer says,

> And the glory which thou gavest me I have given them; that they may be one, even as we are one: I in them, and thou in me, that they may be made perfect in one; John 17:22

The Lord is in you, and you are in him, you are going to be able to speak to him and you will know the truth from the error. I remember one time we went in to talk to someone and he pointed his finger at us; it wasn't right! The spirit of truth is going to stand; it will arise, and you will know inside. He will say,

> I am the way, the truth, and the life: John 14:6

He showed me when I said, "Lord, how am I going to know when things go bad, the deception is so bad?" He said, "You hold a negative up to the light and you see the picture. If someone is in error the light in you is going to show off the darkness in them." He proved deception to me many times. If they don't hear you, the truth isn't in them. Paul kneeled down and prayed; it must have been difficult for him. He knew ahead of time what he was to suffer. I met a woman that was saved in Las Vegas and her testimony was mighty. God told me, "Go outside and pick up the dirt, hold it in the air and I will blow it into all of Nevada for the work of my kingdom." We claimed every Casino on both sides of the street for the Lord, I asked, "Lord which way do you want me to go?" He said, "Claim all of the money!" Then I turned around and drove home.

> For every beast of the forest is mine, and the cattle upon a thousand hills. I know all the fowls of the mountains: and the wild beasts of the field are mine. Psalm 50:10-11

I remember when we went to India Brother Joseph met me in Bombay. It was the highest festivity of the year: the festivity of lights. The Lord told me to bind the powers off of the minds of the people. We couldn't move because there were thousands of people going down the street bowing down to these idols. They were in carts and were walking, thousands of them, down the street. We got into the precession. When we were in it the Spirit of the Lord was on me to bind the powers off of the minds of the people. He Lord was breaking these powers. We did it in Bombay and everywhere we went; the Lord bound these powers. The Spirit the Lord is going to do it.

There was a breaking away of the Hindus coming to God; more than there had ever been. It was the experience of the Lord and He will do it. It also happened in the islands; I did what He said to do. He is preparing us to do things His way. We are going to do what he wants us to do. I believe God is going to prepare us to do His will; by him and through him. In Jesus name! Amen.

ALLOWING GOD'S PERFECT PEACE

This morning I felt the Lord wanted to share this scripture with you. This is a very basic scripture in our ministry down through the years, a part of our foundation that God has laid in our life. It is a part of our life: that we become as He is. And there are a lot of people having struggles right now, even in the midst of us, but there is a way that God has made for us that He will handle it for us if we'll give it to Him. If we keep it, then we're in trouble and we'll keep on believing lies, and the enemy will keep on tearing us up. But God has the answer in His Word because Jesus fulfilled it at the cross.

> Isaiah 26:1 In that day shall this song be sung in the land of Judah; We have a strong city; salvation will *God* appoint *for* walls and bulwarks. 2 Open ye the gates, that the righteous nation which keepeth the truth may enter in. 3 Thou wilt keep *him* in perfect peace, *whose* mind is stayed *on thee*: because he trusteth in thee. 4 Trust ye in the LORD for ever: for in the LORD JEHOVAH *is* everlasting strength: 5 For he bringeth down them that dwell on high; the lofty

city, he layeth it *low*; he layeth it low, *even* to the ground; he bringeth it *even* to the dust. 6 The foot shall tread it down, *even* the feet of the poor, *and* the steps of the needy. 7 The way of the just *is* uprightness: thou, most upright, dost weigh the path of the just. 8 Yea, in the way of thy judgments, O LORD, have we waited for thee; the desire of *our* soul *is* to thy name, and to the remembrance of thee. 9 With my soul have I desired thee in the night; yea, with my spirit within me will I seek thee early: for when thy judgments *are* in the earth, the inhabitants of the world will learn righteousness. 10 Let favour be shewed to the wicked, *yet* will he not learn righteousness: in the land of uprightness will he deal unjustly, and will not behold the majesty of the LORD. 11 LORD, *when* thy hand is lifted up, they will not see: *but* they shall see, and be ashamed for *their* envy at the people; yea, the fire of thine enemies shall devour them. 12 LORD, thou wilt ordain peace for us: for thou also hast wrought all our works in us. 13 O LORD our God, *other* lords beside thee have had dominion over us: *but* by thee only will we make mention of thy name. 14 *They are* dead, they shall not live; *they are* deceased, they shall not rise: therefore hast thou visited and destroyed them, and made all their memory to perish. 15 Thou hast increased the nation, O LORD, thou hast increased the nation: thou art glorified: thou hadst removed *it* far *unto* all the ends of the earth. Isaiah 26:1-15

Jesus paid the price there for us that we might take His Word and believe His Word and accept His Word.

Heaven and earth shall pass away: but my words shall not pass away. Mark 13:31, Luke 21:33

This is how sure His Word is to us if we believe it.

> In that day shall this song be sung in the land of Judah; We have a strong city; salvation will *God* appoint *for* walls and bulwarks. Isaiah 26:1

Now I call "that day" this day, I call it "this day". This is the day that He's going to do it for us. This is the day we're going to sing this song with Judah! He said, "In the land of Judah ..." We're in the land of Judah, aren't we? Amen. We have a strong city, salvation, and will God appoint for walls and bulwarks."

> Open ye the gates, that the righteous nation which keepeth the truth may enter in. Isaiah 26:2

That's what we have to do. We have to open up to the Lord. Now this is a particular people. What kind of people? "A righteous people." That what? "Keepeth the truth." Today we can hardly tell the truth anywhere. The Bible says truth was thrown in the streets. Justice was thrown in the streets. That's what is in this day; and this is the day He's talking about. "Open up the gates and let the righteous nation which keepeth the truth enter in." Now if we don't have the truth, we aren't going to be able to keep the truth, are we? I know a lot of people that are trying to fool around with God, and they want the things of the world, and they want to still be called Christians. That doesn't make us a Christian. What makes us a Christian is keeping the truth. Having Christ in our heart and in our life and doing what His Word says to do and to keep the truth.

> Thou wilt keep *him* in perfect peace, *whose* mind is stayed *on thee*: because he trusteth in thee. Isaiah 26:3

All right, if we keep the truth, if we are righteous, then we are going to be righteous in the righteousness of God. We do not have our own righteousness.

You know we have plans, we say, "Well, this and this, and this is what I'm going to do;" or, "This and this is what I do, and nobody's going to change me;" maybe, "I'm going to do this, and this, and this." And then you say you are Christian? Hmm, it isn't going to work. The compromises that are in the world today are destroying the Christians. There's a parable, and it's called *The Sower* and there's a verse in The Sower that says,

> And some fell among thorns; and the thorns sprang up with it, and choked it. … 14 … and are choked with cares and riches and pleasures of this life, and bring no fruit to perfection. Luke 18:7, 14

That is the condition of the Christian church today. Why? How many of you worry? You worry. Why do you worry? The cares of this life have you to worry. What happens when we have the cares of this life and we allow them to hinder us? We worry and we are not becoming fruitful. What is the fruit that God is after in our lives?

> "The righteous nation which keepeth the truth …" Isaiah 26:1

How many of you have perfect peace?, you need this word. Amen.

> Thou wilt keep *him* in perfect peace, *whose* mind is stayed *on thee*: because he trusteth in thee. Isaiah 26:3

Why is it that we don't have perfect peace? Because our mind is not stayed on Him. Now you're going to say, "How can I keep my mind on the Lord all the time? I can't think about anything else?" That's not what it says. Now I'm going to give you another scripture:

> Trust ye in the LORD for ever: for in the LORD JEHOVAH *is* everlasting strength: For he bringeth down them that dwell on high; the lofty city, he layeth it low; he layeth it low, *even* to the ground; he bringeth it *even* to the dust. Isaiah 26:4-5

Now who do we think we are that God's going to take away a whole city and make it dust? And we're going to stand before Him and declare "I'm going to do my thing my way." Where do you think we're going to be? We're going to become dust, aren't we? We cannot do it our way, God has a better way. Amen. A perfect way, a way for our mind to be stayed in Him, so we can have His perfect peace inside of us.

> … the inhabitants of the world will learn righteousness. Isaiah 26:9

Now the verse 6 says who's going to tread down the city.

> The foot shall tread it down, *even* the feet of the poor, *and* the steps of the needy. Isaiah 26:6

What are they trying to do today with the homeless, the poor, and the needy? A lot of them are on the streets. But what's going to happen to the city? It's going to be trodden down. It's going to go to dust.

> The way of the just *is* uprightness: thou, most upright, dost weigh the path of the just. 8 Yea, in the way of thy judgments, O LORD, have we waited for thee; the desire of *our* soul *is* to thy name, and to the remembrance of thee. 9 With my soul have I desired thee in the night; yea, with my spirit within me will I seek thee early: for when thy judgments *are* in the earth, the inhabitants of the world will learn righteousness. Isaiah 26:7-9

Let's stop on this last verse for a moment, some in this country are trying to say there is no God, taking Him out of our public lives, trying to take Him out of our everything public. But He says, when thy judgments *are* in the earth, the nhabitants of the world will learn righteousness. Now God's judgments are in the earth. He's withheld it to His appointed time, but we're in that appointed time, believe me, when God is going to judge everything we do and say now, if we belong to Him, and if we want Him to be everything in our lives. He cried out,

> With my soul have I desired thee in the night; yea, with my spirit within me will I seek thee early: Isaiah 26:9

You know people are afraid of God's judgments; but God's judgments are to destroy the works of Satan, huh? God's judgment is not against man, it's against Satan and the works of Satan that are in man. He wants to remove it and bring forth His righteousness in each and every one of us. He said, the inhabitants of the world will, not maybe, not perhaps, but will learn what? Righteousness. Do you see the world is in such disarray? It's determined to destroy righteousness, it's determined to destroy truth, it's determined to destroy justice and judgment. But God has determined, by His Word, that His judgment is coming first, and with His judgment is going to come righteousness.

The inhabitants of the world will learn righteousness, how can it be done? God has a lot of ways of doing it, He has a lot of ways of doing it in our own lives, a lot of ways of dealing with us. Because He wants all this junk out of us. He wants us to be pure in His righteousness and in His truth, they that are righteous and keep truth. Now He's not leaving this up to us to change ourselves. He is asking us to let Him do it, He wants to do it, and when He does it, it will be complete and it will be thorough and it will be perfect, right?

Then He goes on to say, "favor will be shewed to the wicked but they will not learn righteousness." Why? Because they are wicked. They want to know God. They don't want to believe that God runs this universe, and they're wicked, they're evil in everything; every part of their being is evil. And God is not doing this for them, because they will never become righteous. But they are going to see judgment and they are going to have to declare that God is doing it. Even if they refuse to accept it, they're going to have to acknowledge it.

> Let favour be shewed to the wicked, *yet* will he not learn righteousness: in the land of uprightness will he deal unjustly, and will not behold the majesty of the LORD. Isaiah 26:10

He will refuse, because in his wickedness he has no desire to know the Lord.

> 11 LORD, *when* thy hand is lifted up, they will not see: *but* they shall see, and be ashamed for *their* envy at the people; yea, the fire of thine enemies shall devour them. Isaiah 26:11

The last laugh is God's, because that wickedness that they're holding on to, God is going to send a fire and burn it up. But in burning it up, they are going to get burned up, because they refuse to acknowledge God and the Lord.

> LORD, thou wilt ordain peace for us: for thou also hast wrought all our works in us. Isaiah 26:12

What's He doing now? He's taking out the works of the flesh. He's taking out the works of the devil. He's taking out all of these things and He's putting His works in us, thou also hast wrought ..." What does that mean? What does the word "wrought" mean? Formed. He is forming us in His righteousness, He is putting His works within us, and sometimes we don't feel that way. We feel all this other stuff, we wonder where His righteousness is, but He's doing something here. He's stirring it up so it can come to the surface, so He can skim it off. Amen... Not our works but His works. He's transforming us.

> And be not conformed to this world: but be ye transformed by the renewing of your mind, that ye may prove what is that good, and acceptable, and perfect, will of God. Romans 12:2

So what is God doing here?

> Thou wilt keep *him* in perfect peace, *whose* mind *is* stayed *on thee*: because he trusteth in thee. Is. 26:3

God's working with our minds right now. Amen.

> O LORD our God, *other* lords beside thee have had dominion over us: *but* by thee only will we make mention of thy name. 14 *They are* dead, they shall not live; *they are* deceased, they shall not rise: therefore hast thou visited and destroyed them, and made all their memory to perish. Isaiah 26:13-14

Let's go back, other lords have had dominion over our lives. What a mess we've made of our lives because we did not choose righteousness. We did not choose truth, so what happened? All these other things came into our lives to take charge of us. Our life's stories are many and varied for everyone but there is one thing that holds true: when Jesus is finished with us, and we allow Him to do this work in us, we're going to be righteous, and we're going to keep the truth, and we're going to have perfect peace.

He's talking about all these other lords. Now we can make a long list of them, can't we? A long list of lords that trouble us all the time, and a lot of them are not even true. These lords come and visit us every day, they torment us, they lie to us, they just tell us all these things, and they are not even true; but they have dominion over us. Why do they have dominion over us? Because we have not given that dominion to God, we've kept it and let it rule us so that other lords besides Him have had dominion over us. I've heard people say, "Oh, well, that's the way I am, if people are going to like me, they're going to like me the way I am, because that's just the way I am." And I look at them and feel sorry for them, because the Lord wants to change our lives and make us like He is. God has a very definite plan to destroy those other lords, but we have a decision to make. Now listen to it, only by the Lord is it going to be done.

> O LORD our God, *other* lords beside thee have had dominion over us: *but* by thee only will we make mention of thy name. Isaiah 26:13

But what? We have to let Him do it, by Him only will we make mention of Jesus' name. We have to bring it to the Lord, and we have to bring it with a determination we're not going to take it back, that we want to be free from it. When we give it to Him this is what He does. He what? He says they're dead. So what happens? He destroys them, they shall not live, they are deceased. When they're deceased, they are dead and buried.

> Therefore Thou hast visited ... and they shall not rise. Isaiah 26:14

If you're dead and buried, you're not going to rise. So, He's made it so positive that there should not be one doubt in your mind at what He can do, huh?

> O LORD our God, *other* lords beside thee have had dominion over us: *but* by thee only will we make mention of thy name. 14 *They are* dead, they shall not live; *they are* deceased, they shall not rise: therefore hast thou visited and destroyed them, and made all their memory to perish. Isaiah 26:13-14

Now that we think is the impossible part, huh? But if we give it to Him, and He destroys it all, then He will accomplished it, and make all their memories to perish.

> Thou hast increased the nation, O LORD, thou hast increased the nation: thou art glorified: thou hadst removed *it* far *unto* all the ends of the earth. Isaiah 26:1-15

I want to tell you that I know the reality of this word, and there are a lot of other people who know the reality of this word. It's mighty, but it's up to us. It's up to us if we want to live like the devil, and we want the devil to rule us, and we want to be tormented day and night, and then say we're Christians; not the Lord. Because He's made the way for us to have perfect peace, and it's not just peace that comes once in a while, Thou wilt keep him, God will keep us, in perfect peace.

I'll pray for you that you'll have peace, and tomorrow if you don't have it, no, remember He destroyed those things and buried them, and they aren't going to rise anymore.

> Knowing this, that our old man is crucified with *him*, that the body of sin might be destroyed, that henceforth we should not serve sin. Romans 6:6

Jesus destroyed the old man of sin. You know, I was trained in a church that talked about sanctification. Then when I started reading the Word the way God gave it to me, I saw something different. They're talking about the old man of sin. Did you ever meet him? Did you ever know him? He's got a lot of Christians bewildered. Do you know what that means? I use to think that, well, it's your carnality that's showing. This used to be an expression in a church I was raised in. If you raised your voice or you said something that they didn't approve of, "Oh, that's your carnality showing!" I got news for you, Jesus said He took it to the cross, He forgave our sins through His shed blood. He destroyed Adam's sin in you, so what did He do? He took it to the cross; it was a curse placed there by the fall of man. Jesus took it to the cross. When we are baptized in water, we have the privilege of carrying "the old man" down there and burying him. He'll let us carry that old man of sin, but He destroyed him on the cross, destroyed his power on the cross for every Christian that will hear it and obey it. You go down into that water, a grave with the Lord, and you bury that old man there. He isn't alive when you go down. He's already dead, he died at the cross. But you have the privilege of burying him, so you know for sure he's not alive.

What a relief it was for me when God opened that scripture because I thought that all my life I was going to have to put up with that old man of sin and walk with Jesus. Thank God it isn't true! We might have a lot of things we need to get rid of, but we have Jesus and He'll get rid of them for us. Amen! He said it is so very important for us to be baptized in water, into Jesus Christ; not into a church, not the Methodist church, not into the Baptist church, not into the Catholic Church, but into Jesus Christ. John's baptism was a baptism of repentance, but the baptism of Jesus is to bring us into Him, and He into us, making us into a quickened spirit. No longer of Adam's race, but a new creature, a new creation formed right there by Jesus Christ as we go down to the cross, and as we go down into the water, the old man is buried there, never to rise again, as long as we allow Jesus Christ to be the Lord and King in His kingdom in our lives.

If we forsake Him, then we are going to go through hell. You're going to go through the horrible things that Satan has for you. But if you hold fast to the Lord and you do what He says, this mighty work that He has given to us is complete in Jesus Christ.

> In Him we live, and move, and have our being. Acts 17:28

He's the one who gives us perfect peace, and it stays with us. He made it possible for us, He ordained it for us. He made it possible for us to be baptized in water, as well, that we might be free from the old man of sin, and that we might live in His peace to destroy all the effects of this life. God has given us the answer - the New Birth. Jesus said to Nicodemus,

> Verily, verily, I say unto thee, Except a man be born of water and of the Spirit, he cannot enter into the kingdom of God. John 3:5

But here He is telling us how He will do the job and finish off what the enemy tries to make us think has to stay inside of us. God removes it if we will let Him, if we don't let Him, we'll go on enjoying it, I think some people enjoy it. I think we need to get determined to let God take the junk, those former lords, out of our lives. The enemy comes, and he'll try to say, "Now, look at you." When you make a mistake, if you get angry, remember God made us like Himself and He gave us a nature like His nature. Adam gave that nature away, didn't he? But Jesus brought it back to us if we want it. It has to be by our own choosing, whether we're free, or whether we allow those lords to tear us up.

Day by day will we allow God to take those former lords away, and totally destroy them, and make their memory to perish so there is no memory left of them? This Word is mighty, and it is real, and God is the one who perfects His people. Jesus perfected it at Calvary, He perfected it as He came up out of that grave. Today His judgment is still on the earth and the inhabitants of the world will learn righteousness. They will learn it through us if we allow Him to finish that work in us so now then we will have His perfect peace. All these things will go from our lives as we rest in Him, He's the Lord of His Word but it's up to us about what we do with it. If we want to carry these things around and complain, it's up to us.

What is so mighty is that He causes the memory of it all to perish? We do not have to live with the junk, we do not have to put up with it if we're willing to let God take it and destroy it. Amen.

How much do we want of His peace? He's ordained for us to have His peace. It's ours, if we want it.

> But if we walk in the light as He is in the light, we have fellowship one with another, and the blood of Jesus Christ His Son, cleanseth us from all sin. 1 John 1:7

He cleanseth us, God Himself cleanseth us. If we make a mistake, if we sin, we come to Him, and we ask Him to forgive us, and immediately God cleanseth us from all sin. I believe if this truth were ministered in the churches as God intended it to be ministered, there would never be a backslider. Because when the devil comes, if we make one mistake or if we commit one little sin, he'll torment us until we commit a million. Then the devil has us hooked. The

Word says, He cleanseth us. Jesus sits at the right hand of the Father ever making intercession for us as the Son of Man. He is still interceding for us to be free from sin, to be free from the powers of Satan. Here in Isaiah it tells the complete work. Here in 1 John He says,

> If we walk in the light, as He is in the light, we have fellowship... 1 John 1:7

What happens? Somebody goes out here, and they commit a sin and then they come among the brethren. What happens? Oh, all at once they are not their brothers, that's right, a very strange feeling is among them. Why? Because they've stepped out of the light and the light in the brethren bothered somebody. All you need to do is step back into the light and ask Jesus to forgive you. Instantly He will forgive us, and then we're walking in the light again. And now we can join the brethren again and fellowship with them. Jesus says He has ordained peace for us and that peace He gives to us. When Jesus came back after He rose from the dead, the first thing He said to His disciples was,

> Peace be unto you. John 20:19

So the Lord is saying, "I've given you My peace"; why do you allow the enemy to take that peace from you?" If you've done something wrong all you do is ask Him to forgive you and that peace returns to you. It's His peace that He's given to us. If we, by our mouths, and by our actions, lose that peace then we need to go back where we lost it and pick it up again. God has it for us, if we let Him give it to us, but we can't keep a mixture. I am very much against some of the things that Christians allow in today's world because they are a compromise; and when there's compromise you might as well tell Jesus, "Good-bye" because when you go over there you're not going to meet with Him. No, you're not! You're not going to be; with your compromises down here, with the wicked who refuse to let Jesus give them perfect peace.

One of the very great signs of the presence of God is His peace. Jesus imparted it immediately to His disciples. When He came to see them after He arose from the dead, He gave them His peace. He's ordained peace for every one of us, and it's ours if we choose it. If we don't choose it, well, I already read what will happen to you, you go to the place of the wicked. The one thing I know, God doesn't want any Christian to be tormented. If you're tormented, you need to get rid of it, give it to the Lord, and His peace will keep you. If you don't believe His Word, don't ask Him to do anything for you. He said to them that believe, all things are possible. He makes it possible, He will do it for us, but we have to be willing to let Him do it. It's ours today if we want it.

I have had two life changing experiences in my life. Two very, very important experiences in my life that changed my life completely and gave me His peace. I was being destroyed, not by my family, but by what I thought. You see, we don't have to be affected by what people say or do, If we're affected by it, we are going to be hurt by it. My mother died when I was 11, leaving me with 5 younger brothers and sisters. My father never cooked, he didn't know anything about children, because he worked away from home most of the time. There were five younger brothers and sisters. Maybe you don't know what younger brothers and sisters do, especially if they don't have a mother, and they have no one in charge of them. Well, they were going to give me a rough time. They said, "Who do you think you are? You can't tell us what to do." And what do you think developed inside of me? A lot of "frustrations and junk."

Then, when I was 16 I gave my life to the Lord, that's when the war really started! The older brothers and sisters said, "She is a religious fanatic!" They took the children, and they took them to another part of the state, and I was not allowed to go and visit them, because I was a "religious fanatic." So they told all kinds of stories about me, and of course it always came back to your ears. By this time I was allowing the effects of these things to destroy me. I had a call; I knew what God wanted me to do, but there was my family. You see, it's wrong if we hold on to a family, when God is trying to separate us from that family, so He can do something in our lives. I didn't have any problems with God; I loved God. But I couldn't serve God because I had all this "stuff" inside of me. And so I was going down, down the other way, because I allowed things people said or did, or what the devil did to destroy me. This was not a joke, it was very serious.

One day the Lord got a hold of me and He told me to give up my family. He said, "I have a family for you that's My family and they will be your family." That day I came about to the end of my life and I knew it. I knew I couldn't go any longer and the Lord literally shook me. He shook me. He said, "I have asked you to give up that family, and you've not obeyed Me. Now I command you to do it." And when He commanded me to do it, I said, "Yes, Lord." I gave it up. I gave it up instantly and the Lord brought out every painful memory, everything that I thought was so horrible, I couldn't tell you what those horrible things were, because He took them and He destroyed them. But I had to let Him do it.

If anything is in our lives that prevent us from allowing Jesus to have full control of our life, we need to get rid of it. If it's a person or if it's things, we need to let go of them. Because I let go of the old family, today and down through the years God has given me a beautiful family – the family of God with all the little children I could love. My family is not my family anymore, they are just kin-folks. They don't effect my life since Jesus took them away, but He had to take them away. If we hang on to things that God is saying to let go of, it will take us and destroy us. But if we let go, He has something far better, if we let Him do it. God has perfect peace for every one of us, if we'll let Him clean house and remove all the things that we still want to hold on to. It's very, very mighty what God will do in a few days. You see, God will do it for all of us. The reason many of us are still wandering around with our problems is because we haven't given them to Him.

Another time I was ministering in Northern California. I had ministered four times that day and I went to my room and had gone to bed. The Lord came into my room and He started performing surgery on my skull. I felt Him open it up and I said to Him, "Lord, what are You doing?" I knew it was the Lord, it was as though I was visualizing what He was doing as He was doing it. I said, "Lord, what are You doing? He said, "I'm taking out what ought not to be there." Then I felt warmth, a very warm-like feeling go through my whole skull. I said, "What are You doing?" He said, "I'm putting My Spirit, My light there, and I'm removing all the darkness." And He sealed the place right there and He said, "I'm sealing that door, so that none of these things will come back." It was a glorious experience, and it's never changed in my life since that day.

Those two experiences transformed my life because the Lord took out those things which the enemy would have used to destroy my life. The Lord told me the conscious mind and the unconscious mind are like a tape recorder. The unconscious mind records everything that we see and hear from the time we are human beings. It's all recorded. All the "junk" you look at on television, all you used to hear on the radio, all the movies you went to, all of this stuff is recorded, right in there. There's not much room left for you to use your brain because it's all polluted. But the Lord said, He's the only one that can erase it, and He'll erase it from us if we let Him. And that's what He did for me, He not only separated me from the people, He took the thought patterns so that I would not allow these things to effect my life. God changed my life so I could tolerate people, so I could live with people and so I could hear Him and obey Him. God wants to do it for every one of us if we desire for Him to change our lives so that we can be an instrument of His love and His peace, His joy, and His righteousness. It's up to us.

I get troubled with our attitudes. We're living beneath what God has given to us when we allow these things to effect us. The Lord has the answer today in His Word: if we want perfect peace, He will give it to us. He'll take away the worry, take away the anxiety. I don't think there was a human being in the world who worried as bad as I did. That's right, from a little child I worried, all I had was worry. I didn't have anything else. But, oh, how wonderful. God loves us so much. He'd take a little old girl down there in Ohio, bare footed and not worth anything, full of worry, who couldn't think straight and transform her life so that Jesus would give her peace. And He will give that peace to you, His peace that doesn't pass away if we walk with Him. If we will let Him give His peace to us it increases in our life, it becomes stronger and stronger.

When I was raising my children I had a condition in my body that was very, very serious. My children, my daughter was 12 and my son was 15, had to put up with me, physically I was a nervous wreck. One day I went to a meeting, and I knew who this man was and I felt to go. As I walked into his meeting, he said to me, "Sister, the Lord is healing you now of a nervous disorder you have had all your life." It went like that, it was gone! From that day to this day I've never had it again, I have God's peace.

I thank God for His love, for His peace, for His caring for us to set us free, and keep us free by His peace. Amen. It's yours this day if you want it. If you want to live with your problems, if you want to live with these things, then live with them, but God has deliverance for you. He has healing, He has peace, a very mighty peace this day if we want it. It's up to us,

> LORD, thou wilt ordain peace for us: for thou also hast wrought all our works in us. 13 O LORD our God, *other* lords beside thee have had dominion over us: *but* by thee only will we make mention of thy name. 14 *They are* dead, they shall not live; *they are* deceased, they shall not rise: therefore hast thou visited and destroyed them, and made all their memory to perish. Isaiah 26:12-13

Lord, cause the memory of it all to perish.

What a mighty God we serve. He's put it in our hands, and what are we going to do with it? Are we going to take heed and hear what He says and let Him change our lives, or are we going to continue in the ways we're going? I'll tell you one thing: I know you'll get worse and not better unless you allow Him to bring His peace and dwell in you. For God has ordained peace for us. His peace, that we might live in His peace, walk in His peace, and become the righteous nation that keeps the truth. Thank God for His Word, we don't need to interpret it, it is what He says it is. I like to give the Word and let the Spirit of the Lord do the talking about it.

Father, we praise You, Jesus, we ask You now to touch every person that hears this word. Jesus, whatever You give us, You impart it to us. Lord, You know the need of every person, each one and everyone, You know the needs this very moment, and Lord, You have purposed for them to have peace. As they that stand before You, look into every heart, every mind, every attitude, everything that is not like You. Jesus, I ask You to move in the midst of this people and set them free. Those who want to be free, Lord, I thank You. This Word You have sent to us, You have given it to us pure, and undefiled, and undiluted. You have given us the straight Word for us, this moment. Now, Lord, I ask You to search every heart, every mind, every person. I ask You now to work that work in each one that is willing to let You do it that they might be free. God, we ask You now to move in the midst of this people, in Jesus name. Amen.

THE PLUMBLINE

The Plumbline, it is time to make a decision. We all have a choice.

We thank you God, for your authority, and your love. We thank you for your justice and your mercy. Precious Lord, I thank you to put into our hearts the training that you have for us. Lord, we thank you now that the principalities have to go, these powers of hell have to go. We need to line up according to the word of God and be filled with Your love and compassion. Lord, You brought us to train us, we belong to You. We aren't going to allow a defiant spirit to rule in our hearts. So, Lord, I thank You to take dominion over every child, man and woman reading. We give You glory for it Jesus in Your wonderful name. Amen.

> Hear me when I call, O God of my righteousness: thou hast enlarged me *when I was* in distress; have mercy upon me, and hear my prayer. Psalm 4:1

> Give ear to my words, O LORD, consider my meditation. 2 Hearken unto the voice of my cry, my King, and my God: for unto thee will I pray. 3 My voice shalt thou hear in the morning, O LORD; in the morning will I direct *my prayer* unto thee, and will look up. Psalm 5:1-3

> O LORD, rebuke me not in thine anger, neither chasten me in thy hot displeasure. 2 Have mercy upon me, O LORD; for I *am* weak: O LORD, heal me; for my bones are vexed. Psalm 6:1-2

> 8 Depart from me, all ye workers of iniquity; for the LORD hath heard the voice of my weeping. 9 The LORD hath heard my supplication; the LORD will receive my prayer. 10 Let all mine enemies be ashamed and sore vexed: let them return *and* be ashamed suddenly. Psalm 6:8-9

> Psalms 7:1 O LORD my God, in thee do I put my trust: save me from all them that persecute me, and deliver me: ... 8 The LORD shall judge the people: judge me, O LORD, according to my righteousness, and according to mine integrity *that is* in me.

Praise the Lord. First we must call upon Him, we ask Him to enlarge us, and have mercy upon us, and hear our prayers. God is telling us what to do so that we can hear Him. We often wonder if He hears our prayers, but when we realize He has set the godly apart for Himself, then we know that He hears us when we pray. Our committal to God has to come first. We come to Him with broken and contrite hearts, we come with an open mind, we ask for forgiveness, and we repent for all the things that we have done. Then, He hears our prayer, then He forgives our sins, then He blots them out. God wants us to know that He hears us when we call, and He will answer as He *gives ear* to our words. God recognizes that we love Him; in the wee hours of the night, we can commune with Him on our beds.

We hear of people who have to go and have to spend a lot of time alone; you know if God is in us we aren't alone, are we? If He's inside of us, we don't have to go somewhere else to talk to Him. You don't have to go out into the field and talk to Him; you can have the privilege of speaking to Him on your bed. God wants us to know Him, He wants to have that intimate relationship with us, and He's telling us

> But know that the LORD hath set apart him that is godly for himself: the LORD will hear when I call unto him. 4 Stand in awe, and sin not: commune with your own heart upon your bed, and be still. Selah. Psalm 4:3-4

Even in the wee hours of the morning, He wakes us up at 3 and 4 in the morning. If He's in you, you don't have to go off somewhere else, you just talk to Him and He'll give your answers, and He'll lead you by His Spirit. One time a lady came to my house, and she said the Lord sent me to take you to my house so the Lord can talk to you. That was new to me, because the Lord talked to me at the clothes line, kitchen sink, scrubbing floors, running the vacuum, making beds; I didn't have to go anywhere else. The Lord said to me, "I didn't send her to tell you to go to her house. If you had gone to her house and spent the night so I could talk to you, it wouldn't have been me talking to you because I talk to you everywhere."

God wants us to have an intimate relationship with Him. Remember, He does hear our prayers, He forgives our sins, and cleanses us from all unrighteousness. And what a joy it is to know that we have peace, that we can lay down in peace, and sleep, and dwell in safety. God has called us to a life of peace and rest; we have to give our life to the Lord in total commitment to Him. God will not meet our needs half way, and we can't come half way to Him, we have to come all the way, He requires total surrender.

What is He taking away from us? Let me tell you, it's kind of one sided, He is taking away sin, and darkness, evil habits, alcohol, drugs, all of the lusts of the flesh, and the pride of the flesh. He's taking it all away and we will be free. So then why do you look back? Don't let the devil torment your mind, instead of this speak, "I'm free, I'm free! The Lord has set me free."

A young woman came from Kansas that had a lot of principalities and powers in her life, she ran away down the road. The young people went to rescue her because anyone could pick her up, and it was pretty evil out there. As the young people ran to get to her, a very tall angel dressed in white, ran after her and tripped her. They caught up with her, and brought her back. This young woman was warring against deliverance; and decided she would run away again. This time a drunken man picked her up and took her to a place where a lot of evil activity was going on. She got away from him and called home. She could have been killed very quickly, but we were interceding for her ever since she walked out the door.

God has a way for you that is His peace, His righteousness, His forgiveness and His healing. We can't play with God or with the devil, because the devil will sure trip you and pull you down fast. Peace comes from God. Joy comes from God. Salvation comes from Him. Love comes from Him. The Lord is calling us into this very beautiful relationship He's talking about in Psalm 4, God's presence and Love in us. God wants us to put our trust in Him.

We all trust our flesh but do we trust God? You are a chosen people and God has chosen you to be 100% in Him. He will train you so He can be 100% in you out there against the evil of this world. You will never know unless you put your trust in Him and let Him show you that He is God. We can do our own thing and God won't stop us because He honors your right to choose. The Lord taught me many years ago that I have no right to interfere with the choice that anyone is making. I have to stand back and let them make it, because they have the right to make it whether it is right or wrong. Sometimes the Holy Ghost says to me, "I'm drawing the plumbline, and this is the last time I'm coming this way." When He says that I have to obey Him, and He has done it. There was a man I knew who had a wife and two children; they used to come to us for help. One night, in the middle of the night, he came for deliverance; He had principalities and powers in his life that were very evil. So we prayed and fasted for Him and the Lord delivered him. His wife, well she wasn't too concerned about God, she said, "When she needed Him she would think of Him." One day the Lord told me to go to their house, the Lord told me I want you to go to that home and I want you to read this scripture to them. I went that night and the Lord gave them the word.

> The Lord repented for this: This also shall not be, saith the Lord God. 7 Thus he shewed me: and, behold, the Lord stood upon a wall *made* by a plumbline, with a plumbline in his hand. 8 And the Lord said unto me, Amos, what seest thou? And I said, A plumbline. Then said the Lord, Behold, I

will set a plumbline in the midst of my people Israel: I will not again pass by them any more: Amos 7:6 -8

My son said to the man's wife, "Do you know something about the Lord?" She said, "I think of the Lord, when I need Him." He said, "What?" I thought this was awful strange that she had no communication with God at all. So that night after we left, the husband walked out of that house never to return again. He divorced his wife, and went his own way, and married someone else. Sometime later he was in a motorcycle accident and ended up in the intensive care unit in the hospital. I went to talk to him, and I believe he had made his peace with God before he passed away. His wife, well, she wasn't going the way God wanted her to because she had no interest in God, except when she needed Him.

Five years later, the wife called me in the middle of the night and said her son was crossing the street at about 3 in the morning and a truck hit him and killed him instantly. The little boy had died, just like his father, I knew the boy in diapers. When he was about 8 years old he carried a Bible around and said, "I'm going to be a preacher." He loved the Lord then; but years went by and now he was 16 years old. He had joined with some devil worshipers, all of his friends were devil worshipers. When we went to the mortuary, his friends were very sad. We said, "Do you know that this boy didn't make it to God? He made a choice, and joined the gangs, and lost his life without God." They said, "Not our friend, this couldn't happen to him." We said, "Do you know your friend is in hell now?" They said, "Not our friend..." We said, "Yes, your friend, because he chose evil rather than the good." I prayed for some of his friends, they were all dressed in black; they didn't look like human beings. It was so terrible. All I could think of was this little boy ... with his Bible. We are responsible to bring our children up in the ways of the Lord. You cannot have God in your life and decide you are going to run your own life, because as surely as you live, you are going to meet up with death, and you are going to lose it.

When God has called us to His way, and we choose our own way, there is trouble. That night when He gave the word that God had put the *plumbline* down and wasn't going to go that way anymore, little did I know what was going to happen to that entire family.

We have choices to make, God will not stop you from your own ways, but your own ways will take you away from God. We must ask Him to take out of us everything that is contrary to His perfect will, and to put His love in us, until everything in us is filled with His love. It is up to us to choose because God made us free, He won't interfere, we have a choice to make. I was in Africa in a village and I met a business man who God had blessed; but then he became greedy. He wasn't satisfied with the blessings of the Lord. He told the Lord he had some deals with people, and the Lord told him it was bribery. He didn't think it was bribery, he thought it was just his friends. This businessman told us a story, one Monday the Lord said to him to get his house in order, because on Saturday he was going to die. God said, "I'm not finished with you." This was Monday and the Lord He told him, "You get everything straight, and ask everyone to forgive you." The businessman remembered one woman that had a lot of hate against him. He went to see her and said, "I want you to forgive me." She threw hot soup in his face, and he wondered what he was going to do. Eventually he got her to listen and forgive him. He only had one week to save his life. God said, "Get your house in order." On Saturday he was healthy, there was nothing wrong with him, but he died. Sunday morning his family brought him to the His Stripes Hospital — dead, a corpse. There was nothing they could do; they didn't have time for a corpse.

The doctor had heard the story of Lazarus in his Sunday school class, as he listened the Lord said, "You take this corpse and bring him to your hospital." His head nurse said, "This man's dead, he's a corpse." The doctor said, "Put an IV in him." His head nurse said, "He doesn't have any veins." The doctor said, "Put it where you know the veins are." He was dead for four days, still the head nurse put him in the bed as the doctor ordered. The doctor went home to rest for a little while, he felt very tired and fell asleep, then the Lord took him by the Spirit to follow the businessman that had died. The businessman went into the heavens. They opened up the book of life to see if his name was written in it. God said, "I have four counts against you." So, they came with a bottle and a brush, in that bottle was the blood of Jesus. They took that brush and washed away the four charges against him. He stood there and didn't know what was going to happen because he wasn't sure the Lord had forgiven him. The Lord washed it away right in front of him.

The businessman saw a friend behind him who was a Christian and he heard them say, "Depart from me, I never knew you." Others came and He said, "Depart from me, I never knew you." When he got to a certain point the Lord told him, "You have to go back." The doctor heard what the Lord was saying to this man. The Lord took him back to his bedroom. The doctor waited for the businessman to return. Every day, he thought he would come back and find this man awake but it wasn't so, four days went by. On the fourth day, there were tears coming down his eyes, that was the first sign of life. The Lord restored him for one purpose, God said, "Go and tell my people there's no purgatory. There's heaven and hell. You choose one or the other, go and warn my people." Choices we make determine where we are going to live for eternity; there are only two places to go. When I was 16 I had gone so far away from God that the Lord shook me over hell. He opened hell up and He said to me, "If you don't serve me, this is where you will go." And that's as straight as it is; if we don't serve Him, that's where we're going to go. But if we serve Him think of what God is going to give to us in exchange.

How can we resist His love, and that which He has given to us? Do we prefer darkness in our lives? He can send us to hell; or are we willing to let Him clean our houses, and fill us with His love until our being is saturated with the love of God. I'm not a hell fire preacher but I know very well what hell is like. I know the price that we have to pay if we don't walk with God with all our heart. The people who don't want to help the poor; one day before very long, are going to stand before God. God is not going to ask them how many thousands of souls they have brought into the kingdom. He is going to ask

> For I was an hungred, and ye gave me no meat: I was thirsty, and ye gave me no drink: 43 I was a stranger, and ye took me not in: naked, and ye clothed me not: sick, and in prison, and ye visited me not. Matthew 25:42-43

I don't care how big we are, if we're not doing the command of the Lord we're going to miss it.

> *Is it* not to deal thy bread to the hungry, and that thou bring the poor that are cast out to thy house? when thou seest the naked, that thou cover him; and that thou hide not thyself from thine own flesh? Isaiah 58:7

Isaiah 58 is very loud and clear, and God requires it of us. Maybe you don't want to do it, but if you love God, it's in your heart to meet the needs of others. There's only one outlet on this earth and that is brotherly kindness — loving one another, serving one another, helping the poor, meeting the needs that Jesus laid before us in the Gospels. That which Jesus did, He requires of us to do.

We have a straight line – a plumbline. I don't mind walking that line, because it's a line of peace, joy, righteousness, and holiness with the Lord. We need this understanding: God is calling a people who He can love and sing to, who He can rejoice over as we walk and run in His love to the nations of the world. What God has in store for us is very awesome as we empty out ourselves and let His love fill us.

In the story of the businessman, the one thing that was missing with a woman that was sent to hell was that she didn't have God's love, that was the only thing that was against her. If the love of the world is in us, then the love of the Father isn't. If we love the Father, the love of the world isn't in us. God is drawing a straight line in our lives so He can fill us and let His love will flow through us. God will make the way for us, we don't have to make it for ourselves, and if we make it for ourselves we are going to miss it. If we give our way to God, God will direct it, and we will have that peace, joy, and righteousness. It's better to have Jesus in charge of our lives. It is better to have His love and glory and His kingdom operating in us.

We have a choice to make. If we chose Him, we shall eternally be blessed by Him, and live in His kingdom forever. If we don't choose Him, we will be damned forever. It's not a little thing, we need to choose Him. He loves us; He doesn't want us to go to the place where the devil is going. He wants us to go to the place that He has prepared and for us. He won't force us, only compel us except by His love to draw us unto Him. His love compels us to follow Him.

I want to leave these words with you, "Choose Him, there isn't anything lacking in what He wants for us if we will but follow Him. God has given us so much, if we will just hear what He's saying. We don't have to entangle ourselves with other things and it's so clear and simple and mighty, if we receive it. God will impart it to you if you allow Him, be willing to walk that path of liberty, peace, and joy, righteousness, and holiness."

Father, we thank You for this word. Jesus, we thank you that you don't say one thing and do another; neither do you want us saying one thing and doing something else. Lord, speak to our hearts, let us know your great love and provision that we might take this Gospel of the Kingdom of Jesus Christ into all the world, that we might be witnesses to all nations. So, that you Lord, can return again unto your people. Lord Jesus, speak your love, your comfort, and your strength to us. Lord let your spirit flow through us, moving in our lives, so that we choose to walk in the Spirit of Life. Lord Jesus, bring life that we may live throughout all eternity. We rejoice in everything you have done for us, for you said you will not hold anyone guiltless who turned away from Christ or rejected Him. Lord, we thank you for the truth, and the truth will make us free. Jesus, I thank you for ears to hear, and a heart to receive, and a heart to obey, in Jesus name. Amen.

Taken from the message "The Plumbline – It is Time to Make a Decision - We All Have a Choice" by Rev. Agnes I. Numer

Eric Etter receiving high school diploma from Agnes I. Numer

LORD, YOU HAVE ORDAINED PEACE FOR US

LORD, thou wilt ordain peace for us: for thou also hast wrought all our works in us. 13 O LORD our God, *other* lords beside thee have had dominion over us: *but* by thee only will we make mention of thy name. 14 *They are* dead, they shall not live; *they are* deceased, they shall not rise: therefore hast thou visited and destroyed them, and made all their memory to perish. Isaiah 26:12-14

Lord, thou wilt ordain peace for us: why does he say it that way? He said it because He willed it, He desires it for us; but it is up to us to receive it. He said, "I will that you have peace." If He has ordained peace for us, then we have to receive that peace. He has also *wrought,* which is to beat out or shape, all of our works in us; everything that we are or He can make us.

It is not our will that gives us power to have peace, we can only have it if we can accept it. If we worry instead of accepting His peace, then we will not have peace. Other lords rob us of that peace.

> Peace I leave with you, my peace I give unto you: John 14:27

Jesus said, I give my peace to you; but if we do not receive it, how can we have it? If you have other lords in your life you will not have peace in your life.

Before we can have God's peace we have to clean house by acknowledging the other lords, and then by renouncing them.

> O LORD our God, *other* lords beside thee have had dominion over us: *but* by thee only will we make mention of thy name. Isaiah 26:13

We are not going to make mention of those other lords any more, we are going to renounce them, we will formally declare that we have abandoned them. And then ... we don't mention them anymore. God said,

> *They are* dead, they shall not live; *they are* deceased, they shall not rise: therefore hast thou visited and destroyed them, and made all their memory to perish. Isaiah 26:14

God took those former lords and destroyed them! If we will just allow Jesus to take those lords and destroy them God will cause their memory to perish. We will not remember the horrible things anymore, we will have His peace. He will change our lives and gives us His peace. Jesus said to the storm

Peace, be still. And the wind ceased, and there was a great calm. Mark 4:39

The Holy Spirit gave His peace through the disciples when they ministered to the people. If the people received their words then peace remained. If the people rejected their words, then Jesus said,

> And if the house be worthy, let your peace come upon it: but if it be not worthy, let your peace return to you. And whosoever shall not receive you, nor hear your words, when ye depart out of that house or city, shake off the dust of your feet. Mat. 10:13-14

Jesus gives us this peace today. People must receive truth in order for their lives to change, if they reject the truth, they will not have peace anymore.

If you lose your peace, ask yourself where you were when you lost it, what were you doing? What was God telling you to do? Go back to that place and find your peace again. God says,

> Peace I leave with you, my peace I give unto you: not as the world giveth, give I unto you. Let not your heart be troubled, John 14:27

> I am the light of the world: he that followeth me shall not walk in darkness, but shall have the light of life. John 8:12

If you are out somewhere and you do not feel God's peace; stop and ask God what happened? Obey God, you do not want to be where God is not. We have to have perfect peace to move forward and do what God wants us to do. If we have both truth and deception we have confusion. How are we going to know what we are supposed to do? How will we lead others?

Does the church realize we can be filled with His perfect peace? The world wants their ways, but Jesus wants us to come to the light. If others reject the truth they will be deceived, but we will stand with boldness and we will have His perfect peace. Sometimes when the devil speaks to us he tries to make us doubt; do not listen to him! Tell him, "You do not live in me anymore!" You do not need to argue with the devil, you do not need to be afraid. God's word is in us and He is the one that keeps us from fear. There is no law against truth, love, and peace: no one and no law can take it from you. When we believe God's word then the devil cannot have any effect on us. Testing will come and that is when we must stand on God's word; He will use the testing to make us strong. When Jesus was tested He said, "It is written." Matthew 4:4 He is victor over the enemy and so are we because we believe in His truth. God ordained peace for us, He has taken us through, we have stood in the truth, and now God can use us to help someone else.

Oh Lord our God, only by thee will we make mention of thy name, the former lords are dead, if they are deceased, they are dead. If we try to dig up the past, we are digging up dead bodies. They are gone. As we allow God to take His perfect peace in us, the former lords no longer live. He ordained it, He desires it and He willed it for us. Whatever is in His will is yours, what are you going to do with it?

Where do we get the truth? From His word. How do you know you have the truth? Jesus said,

> I am the way, the truth, and the life: no man cometh unto the Father, but by me. John 14:6

He is the Way back the Father. There is no other way. In the new birth the Prince of Peace comes to live inside of us. If we confess our sins He will forgive us and give us His peace, His life, His love, and fill us with His light. Then we realize our sins are gone and perfect peace is there. His written word must be strong in us! Jesus is the Living Word in us.

God wants to use you to help others. After He has brought this peace in your life He wants to use you as a light in this world for others.

> Ye are the light of the world. A city that is set on an hill cannot be hid. 15 Neither do men light a candle, and put it under a bushel, but on a candlestick; and it giveth light unto all that are in the house. 16 Let your light so shine before men, that they may see your good works, and glorify your Father which is in heaven. Matthew 5:14-16

Discern the need that they have, the area of their lives that does not have peace. Let them read Isaiah 26 and know that this is God's will for them; and that Jesus died and rose again that they may have peace and eternal life.

Pray with them believing for this creative miracle in their minds, their emotions, and their spirits. God will heal their brokenness and He will visit those areas of torment and bring peace. He will show them how to allow Him to make them into a man or woman of God. Show them to read His word and get to know him.

Encourage them to stay away and not go places or do things where those former lords had control.

This is something God does, only God can bring this kind of peace, a peace that passes understanding. We cannot deliver someone from torment, only He can. And when He does oh the glory! Oh the joy! We are set free.

God wills peace for you, He desires it for you, are you ready to receive His peace now?

Taken from the message "Isaiah 26" by Rev. Agnes I. Numer

Agnes I Numer, Dr Lilibeth Say, Teresa Skinner (1990)

FAITH WORKETH BY LOVE

> For we through the Spirit wait for the hope of righteousness by faith. Galatians 5:5

Father, we praise you, we thank you for your hallowed presence, we thank you for honoring us with your presence. Lord, we thank you for honoring us to be your servants to obey you. Today Jesus, speak to our hearts, make plain the Word before us that we might write it on our hearts so that we might not sin against you. We thank you for the Living Word, thank you Jesus. Bless this people, Jesus, with your richest blessings. Oh God, you know every need and you're the One that can meet those needs. We thank you Lord Jesus. Father, we thank you for the Word of God. We thank you now for what you're doing in each of our lives, preparing us to be sent by you wherever you choose for us to go. We thank you, Jesus. Lord, let this Word be what you want it to be to each of us and we magnify your name and give you glory in Jesus name. Amen.

Let's turn to Galatians chapter 5. I think this chapter is very important to each of our lives. The Lord spoke to me in the wee hours of the morning concerning it.

> Galatians 5:1 Stand fast therefore in the liberty wherewith Christ hath made us free, and be not entangled again with the yoke of bondage. 2 Behold, I Paul say unto you, that if ye be circumcised, Christ shall profit you nothing. 3 For I testify again to every man that is circumcised, that he is a debtor to do the whole law. 4 Christ is become of no effect unto you, whosoever of you are justified by the law; ye are fallen from grace. 5 For we through the Spirit wait for the hope of righteousness by faith. 6 For in Jesus Christ neither circumcision availeth any thing, nor uncircumcision; but faith which worketh by love. 7 Ye did run well; who did hinder you that ye should not obey the truth? 8 This persuasion *cometh* not of him that calleth you. 9 A little leaven leaveneth the whole lump. 10 I have confidence in you through the Lord, that ye will be none otherwise minded: but he that troubleth you shall bear his judgment, whosoever he be. 11 And I, brethren, if I yet preach circumcision, why do I yet suffer persecution? Then is the offense of the cross ceased. 12 I would they were even cut off which trouble you. 13 For, brethren, ye have been called unto liberty; only *use* not liberty for an occasion to the flesh, but by love serve one another. 14 For all the law is fulfilled in one word, *even* in this; Thou shall love thy neighbor as thyself. 15 But if ye bite and devour one another, take heed that ye be not consumed one of another. 16 *This* I say then, Walk in the Spirit, and ye shall not fulfill the lust of the flesh. 17 For the flesh lusteth against the Spirit, and the Spirit against the flesh: and these are contrary the one to the other: so that ye cannot do the things that ye would. 18 But

if ye be led of the Spirit, ye are not under the law. 19 Now the works of the flesh are manifest, which are *these*; adultery, fornication, uncleanness, lasciviousness, 20 Idolatry, witchcraft, hatred, variance, amulations, wrath, strife, seditions, heresies, 21 Envyings, murders, drunkenness, revellings, and such like: of the which I tell you before, as I have also told you in time past, that they which do so such things shall not inherit the kingdom of God. 22 But the fruit of the Spirit is love, joy, peace, longsuffering, gentleness, goodness, faith, 23 Meekness, temperance: against such there is no law. 24 And they that are Christ's have crucified the flesh with the affections and lusts. 25 If we live in the Spirit, let us also walk in the Spirit. 26 Let us not be desirous of vain glory, provoking one another, envying one another. Galatians 5:1-26

Isn't that a powerful word?

For we through the Spirit wait for the hope of righteousness by faith. Galatians 5:5

We are made righteous in Christ with His righteousness, there's one little word here; did you catch it? Love. Sometimes by the way we act toward one another we wouldn't know that we love one another. I praise the Lord for the love of God. God is changing our lives because we have His love, we also have a lot of things still in our lives that war against His love. Isn't this true? So what has to happen here? Something has to change, His love isn't going to change so we have to change, we have to allow Him to change us. Now, I know as human beings we are very sensitive. If we're in the flesh we're even more sensitive, and if we're looking for trouble, we find it. You find it even among those who love you because they're not quite out of the woods themselves.

What Paul is saying is very plain. In the first place there is only one way that our love is going to operate and His faith operate in us. He's talking about *without works*, our faith is no good to us. Now, there are a lot of *works* in the world today and they are by faith, but not really by *faith*, they call it faith but they organize everything and there's no room for God to organize anything. They call their works *by faith*; but God has a way by His Spirit that He wants to lead us, not under the law, but by grace. Now I think that grace is tolerant, isn't it? It's not like the law. Sometimes we get like the law don't we? And we don't bend in any direction, we kind of get like, "This is the way it is you know." But grace comes along and says, "Let's have some mercy on it." Then we learn not everybody is at the same spiritual level as we are.

So God is good, He doesn't measure us by ourselves or one another, He measures us by His light. We're walking in His light, not in our lights, you're not walking in my light, I'm not walking in your light, we're walking in the light of the Lord. He's giving it to you and then you have to walk in it. There are certain things that we need to do as we're walking with Jesus. Paul said,

> If we live in the Spirit, let us also walk in the Spirit.
> Galatians 5:25

If we live in the spirit, then we must walk in the Spirit, and sometimes our flesh gets in the way, or we get confused. The Lord is very clear here, what is of the Spirit and what is not of the Spirit. If we get over in this little territory that isn't of

His Spirit we need to recognize it immediately and do something about it.

> But if ye be led of the Spirit, ye are not under the law.
> Galatians 5:18

He said if we're led by the Spirit, we're under grace, we're not under the law. We have to remember we're not under the law. Maybe our brothers and sisters don't see things exactly the way we see them, but remember they're not walking in your light, they're walking in the light that He has given to them. Now remember when we come to Jesus He changes our life, He brings us to His kingdom. In Him is life and when we allow Him to come into our lives, we are forgiven of our sins, and then something happens inside of us.

We're in a new kingdom, we're not under the law, but we're under grace, and grace abounds for us. We have to be careful that we're not trying to pull somebody else the way we want them to go; but we direct them to Christ for it is Christ in us that's the hope of glory. Not how somebody thinks about it, not how we think about it, but it's Jesus in us, He's the one that brings His Spirit and causes us to walk in His Spirit. When we walk in His Spirit the word says we don't fulfill the things of the flesh. We need to realize that He's saying two things, He's saying the works of the flesh are one thing, but the fruit of the Spirit is love. God is saying to us, "Walk away as far as you can go from the works of the flesh; go straight to the cross and you go to Jesus." In your heart you have to have a determination that you are going to separate yourself from that flesh. You are not going to allow the flesh to rule but you are going before the cross; you are going to give it to Jesus and you are determined you want to be free. Now He said, "Don't use that freedom for an occasion of the flesh," sometimes we do but God will speak to us about it.

> For the law of the Spirit of life in Christ Jesus hath made me free from the law of sin and death. Romans 8:2

He said if we're led by the Spirit we're under a new law, that law which we have by the Spirit of God under grace, is the law of the Spirit of life in Christ Jesus. It has made us free from the laws of sin and death. Many Christians are still living under the laws of sin and death, they do not realize that there's a new law that's operating inside of them. They need to allow Jesus to take care of the things that need to be done. We have a new law in us and that law is the law of the Spirit of Life in Christ Jesus. Now with this law there's a fruit that comes from this new relationship that we have with Jesus.

> But the fruit of the Spirit is love, joy, peace, longsuffering, gentleness, goodness, faith, Meekness, temperance: against such there is no law. Galatians 5:22

Remember that, there is no law against it. There are laws against the works of the flesh, if we get out there doing the works of the flesh we're liable to end up in prison; but not with the laws of the Spirit of Life. We are free from the law of sin and death, we're not under that law. We're not out there sinning like the world does, but we have to remember that there's a way we have to walk. We have to walk in the spirit. There are things that the Lord has to do. A lot of deliverance must come to us, isn't that right? We have to be set free from the old laws of sin and death.

Now when we're water baptized, the Bible says the old man is buried, isn't that exciting? I was raised a Nazarene and you had to fight the old man all the days of your life. But one day the Lord showed me it wasn't true. It was very mighty how He showed it to me. I was ministering on water baptism and all of a sudden the Lord took me into a realm that I knew nothing about. The meeting lasted two whole hours. He took me in to the watery grave with Him and He showed me what it meant to be baptized in water into His death. We carry the old man right there, we bury him, and he's no longer a part of us. Then we realize we came up a new creature, a new creation, with a new life in us, and the old things had passed away. The law is fulfilled, but grace comes there with us. As the Lord gave me this experience He took me down; He took the keys away from Satan, and handed them to me. It was an awesome time, the glory and presence of the Lord filled the living room when He began to reveal His word as it is, as it is to us today.

We don't have to struggle with the old man of sin, we have to get rid of him by water baptism. Give him to Jesus and He buries it down there, you see, we can't get forgiveness for it because we didn't commit it. We can take the old man of sin and bury him, the responsibility is then ours and we can't blame it on the old man of sin. After water baptism if there are things in our life we have to remember we're responsible to get them out and get rid of them. The old man, is that sinful nature, is dead and buried so we can't blame him any more. Christians blame the old sinful nature if they do something wrong, but it doesn't work because the word says that sinful nature is dead and buried through water baptism and now you are accountable and you will have to stand before God.

> And this is love, that we walk after his commandments. 2 John 1:6

God said, "Here I have a new walk for you, it's a walk in the Spirit. If you live in the Spirit then you walk in the Spirit."

> This I say then, Walk in the Spirit, and ye shall not fulfil the lust of the flesh. Galatians 5:16

What happens to a lot of people? They don't realize what Jesus has done for them. They go around carrying it all, and think they have to because the old man is there, and there's nothing we can do about it. But this is not true, he's not there; so we're responsible to get rid of it ourselves. If we get some hangovers of the old life then we better cut them off and say, "Lord, I don't want them, I want to walk in the Spirit, I want to live in the Spirit, I want the Spirit of the Lord to have His way in me." If we walk in the Spirit then we're walking in His love because the fruit of His Spirit is love.

You know when you come to Jesus, how full of love you feel? So mighty is that love when you turn your life over to Him, and then His joy and His peace comes you. You have new life, you're a new creature in Christ Jesus, then let's see how fast you can get rid of the works of the flesh. People make mistakes, and maybe they don't talk to you the way they ought to, but they have to answer to God for it, not you. But the way you take it matters, you will have to answer to God for it. We have to be careful that we're not effected by people, we are all human beings and we are all learning how to walk in the Spirit. We don't want to be contaminated with the works of man, we want to be free in the love of God, and know that Jesus provides that love for you by His Spirit so that His pure love can flow, and you can be free, God's love is the answer.

Sometimes we get busy, we forget that the natural and the spiritual have to flow together or we have a collusion, don't we? What's the matter today in a world of Christianity? We got so spiritual that we forgot the natural. God said we have to bring the spiritual into the natural so that the natural becomes spiritual and the spiritual becomes natural. Only then, can we flow together without bumping against one another. We flow together because we're in the Spirit of God. The most important training is to teach us to flow by the Spirit of God. The Lord spoke this to me, "If you just tell them to pray for this food and the people that are receiving it then God is going to work with them." They're going to know, you won't want to take a nap in between because God's strength and joy will be with you. As you're praying for them God's love is going out to them.

Did you know that if a person doesn't have anybody to pray for them God can't save them? Do you know why? Because God has to be asked to save them, there has to be someone who cares enough to pray for them because God will not just go out and force anybody to come to Him. Someone has to care enough to be the intercessor that will draw them to God.

We're living in an awesome time. We're living in a time when the gathering of the nations is coming before God. We have to be faithful in bringing this gospel of the kingdom of Jesus Christ to the nations of the world. There's a world out there in denominationalism, Moslem, Muslim, Hinduism, Buddhism, Atheism, and they don't know Jesus. This is the day the Lord is pouring out His Spirit. This is the day that He's training us to flow by His Spirit, filling us with His love because that love is what is going to change the lives of people.

God is calling us to be trained by His Spirit so that when we go out there God's love is going to draw them. God's peace, His joy, His righteousness will be in us there to draw them unto Him. The world is looking for God's love, I feel that love so much. The Lord says, "Let us live in the Spirit and let us walk in the spirit to show forth His love, His peace, His joy, longsuffering, gentleness, goodness, faith, meekness, and temperance." This I like very much; they can't arrest you for that. There's no law against it. They can't take it from you, so walk in it.

It's so mighty what God is doing, we must all be trained by the Spirit of the Lord. The sooner we allow God to train us in the little things, the sooner He will give us bigger jobs to do. I know we think we are all ready to go out, but we aren't quite ready yet. We think we are, maybe we have to peel a few more potatoes, or scrub a few more floors, or wash a few more dishes. Whatever it is that God is training you in to prepare you, the most important is shedding the old man, and allowing God's love to come inside of us. We're not going to be envious and jealous of one another, neither are we going to bite and devour one another, but we have to walk in His love.

> And this is love, that we walk after his commandments. 2 John 1:6

It seems like every once in a while we kind of need to be remembering that Jesus loves us. But this love which He gives to us is not for us. What is it for? If we keep it, it's not any good to us. What do we have to do? We give it away. How do we give it? By going to church on Sunday? No, there's only one way, through *brotherly kindness*. If you have a brother in need, this ministry is a great example of God's love, know we did not do it, God did it. Today, great and mighty things are happening and we have a part in it, you have a part in it. God didn't call you just to be here, He called you to fill you with His love and compassion, He called you to do whatever He needs you to do, He called to change your life so that together we can reach out to fill the needs of others.

We're under a new law, the law of His love and a new life in Christ Jesus, I think we need to take hold of it, sometimes we're so wrapped up in ourselves that we miss it. God wants us to look beyond ourselves. You know the devil said to me one time, "How are you going to minister to people, look at your life." I said, "I'm very aware of it, Satan." I got up in the middle of the floor and I stomped my feet at him and I said, "Devil, I'm going to obey the Lord, I'm going to minister to people, and God is going to take care of me!" He never bothered me again with it because one thing he knew for sure, I meant business and he wasn't going to stop me. He knew I wasn't going to listen to him, I took a stand. I took a stand and I meant every word of it.

Now we can be determined to allow God to train us to flow by His Spirit, and in His love, and bring that love to the world. It isn't how we handle it, it's how we allow Him, He is going to do it. Amen. We may use our psychology or philosophies but they aren't going to work. The only way that it is going to work is with His love, God's love is going to do it. God has to perfect us in that love because when we come to Him with our whole hearts, and we give our whole lives to Him, then something is going to happen to us. We come under a new law.

One day I was teaching and all at once this second verse jumped right out at me and I never saw it like this before.

> There is therefore now no condemnation to them which are in Christ Jesus, who walk not after the flesh, but after the Spirit. 2 For the law of the Spirit of life in Christ Jesus hath made me free from the law of sin and death. Romans 8:1-2

"Hath made me free," hath made us free, it jumped right out at me, after years and years of reading this word, and it took hold of me. I said, "Thank you, Jesus. We're not under the law of sin and death, we're under the new law of *the Spirit of life in Christ Jesus*." His love in us as we walk in the Spirit we fulfill the things of the spirit.

Only through brotherly kindness can the world know his love. God has given us so much, and He wants to prepare us so that we will walk in the truth, live in the truth, obey the truth, and the truth will set us free.

How much do we want of Him? How much do we want to walk by His Spirit? I would suggest you read this again, if you have a few minutes, let it penetrate through you. Then get a determination that you're not going to walk in the flesh, but you're going to walk in the Spirit so that the Lord can use you to minister His love to the world out there. It's real, it's mighty, and it's wonderful. We have to give our all to Him, if we give our all to Him He gives His all to us, it's up to us.

Praise God for His love, for the marvelous provision of that love that we have to give it, we have to share it. It's so wonderful the provision that God has made for us inside. There's a scripture in 2 Peter 1:4-9 that tells us about how He processes our lives to bring His love into our lives. The processing brings us into godliness, and after godliness it brings us into brotherly kindness, and after brotherly kindness, He brings us into His love transforming of our lives. I said, "Lord, why is brotherly kindness named here?" He said "Only through brotherly kindness can the world know His love." Isaiah 58 is the demonstration of the kingdom of God and His love. When He gives us this revelation it changes our lives. And through this demonstration of God's love men and women come to God. It's not what we do, it's what He does through the changing of their lives.

Are we willing to let Him do it or are we going to let our flesh arise and hinder? If we let our flesh die and really allow Him to change our lives then we're going to see some marvelous things happening, some things we've never seen in all our lives. God is revealing mighty things in this hour to change the lives of the multitudes, they're simple things, they're not the bright things that we would think of; but they're things we would never think of that God is using to change lives. The simple things, the simple words that He would say that we would not think of; God is bringing forth through a people trained by the spirit to set others free.

> The LORD thy God in the midst of thee is mighty; he will save, he will rejoice over thee with joy; he will rest in his love, he will joy over thee with singing. Zephaniah 3:17

What a mighty God we serve! Would you like to have the Lord sing to you? I was struck with awe as I read that scripture and I said, "God, that You would sing to me?" We are talking about singing to Him, but He wants to sing to us with joy.

I was going through an experience; in fact I was dying in a hospital when the Lord gave me this scripture. As the doctors gave me up, the Lord gave me that scripture. It's awesome to know God is singing to you, He loves you so much, because you love Him, because you obey Him, He wants to sing to you, and let you know how much He loves you. The doctors gave me up and the devil came to snatch my life. Every time he came to snatch my life, the Lord gave me that scripture.

> The Lord thy God in the midst of thee is mighty, Zephaniah 3:17

He gave me the whole verse not just the first part of it, but all of it. I recognized that He had the power over the devil, and that it wasn't my time to go, He brought life back into my body. God wants us to get close to Him so that He can demonstrate His love to us. We're not worthy, but we're not going on our worthiness, we're going on His love. That is our privilege to allow the Lord to fill us with His love.

Father, we thank you, we thank you for your love. Jesus, we thank you for the Spirit of God. Lord, we pray that even today you are enlightening our understanding that we might come a little closer and allow you to remove the works of the flesh from our lives, that we might be a light unto others and that they may know that you love them.

We thank you for the Living Word, we thank you for the written word. We thank you Jesus, that you placed your love within us by your Spirit that we might walk in it, live in it, move in it, and Lord, through your love, help others be won by you. We give you glory Lord, let your blessings come to each and every one of us, cause us to desire to be filled with your love, compassion, your gentleness, and your kindness. We ask this in your wonderful name Jesus and for your glory. Amen.

Gary Beaton and Agnes I. Numer

COME UP HIGHER IN HIS LOVE

Our human love does not compare with God's love. Paul was well pleased with the Philippians, and he loved them very dearly. He stated that they were his joy and crown, and he said,

> … so stand fast in the Lord … Philippians 4:1

He gave instructions to them, but he also is saying to pray:

> The Lord is at hand. 6 Be careful for nothing; but in every thing by prayer and supplication with thanksgiving let your requests be made known unto God. 7 And the peace of God, which passeth all understanding, shall keep your hearts and minds through Christ Jesus. Philippians 4:5-7

I believe we need to renew these words in our own lives, it's not so easy because some are more processed than others; some have been through the fire a little more and have a lot of stuff burned out, and some haven't had it yet. Paul was kind of allowing all of this.

> Philippians 4:1 Therefore, my brethren dearly beloved and longed for, my joy and crown, so stand fast in the Lord, *my* dearly beloved. 2 I beseech Euodias, and beseech Syntyche, that they be of the same mind in the Lord. 3 And I intreat thee also, true yokefellow, help those women which laboured with me in the gospel, with Clement also, and *with* other my fellowlabourers, whose names *are* in the book of life. 4 Rejoice in the Lord always: *and* again I say, Rejoice. 5 Let your moderation be known unto all men. The Lord *is* at hand. 6 Be careful for nothing; but in every thing by prayer and supplication with thanksgiving let your requests be made known unto God. 7 And the peace of God, which passeth all understanding, shall keep your hearts and minds through Christ Jesus. 8 Finally, brethren, whatsoever things *are* true, whatsoever things *are* honest, whatsoever things *are* just, whatsoever things *are* pure, whatsoever things *are* lovely, whatsoever things *are* of good report; if *there be* any virtue, and if *there be* any praise, think on these things. 9 Those things, which ye have both learned, and received, and heard, and seen in me, do: and the God of peace shall be with you. 10 But I rejoiced in the Lord greatly, that now at the last your care of me hath flourished again; wherein ye were also careful, but ye lacked opportunity. 11 Not that I speak in respect of want: for I have learned, in whatsoever state I am, *therewith* to be content. 12 I know both how to be abased, and I know how to abound: every where and in all things I am instructed both to be full and to be hungry, both to abound and to suffer need. 13 I can do all things through Christ which strengtheneth me. 14 Notwithstanding ye have well done, that ye did

communicate with my affliction. 15 Now ye Philippians know also, that in the beginning of the gospel, when I departed from Macedonia, no church communicated with me as concerning giving and receiving, but ye only. Philippians 4:1-15

God's love is so mighty, He wants to do so much in our lives that will change our lives. He wants to remove that which is human in nature, and He wants to let God's peace come and keep our hearts and minds through Him. There are times when we are moved by circumstances. The Lord wants to change us so that we can be like Him, I truly believe that God wants to so transform our lives with His love so that we do not have the interference of human love to realize that God's love surpasses anything else. God is doing the impossible in every one of our lives so that we can go forth in His love so that His love is going to reach the world. I do not believe that human love mixed with God's love is perfect; I believe it is imperfect. But what God wants to do for us is to remove the carnal love and put in a love for others so that we will not be affected by circumstances. For example, if we love somebody helping someone, and they do something very bad against us, then we are hurt and we go on the defensive. But God is saying,

> And the peace of God, which passeth all understanding, shall keep your hearts and minds through Christ Jesus. Philippians 4:7

> Charity suffereth long, *and* is kind; charity envieth not; charity vaunteth not itself, is not puffed up, 5 Doth not behave itself unseemly, seeketh not her own, is not easily provoked, thinketh no evil; 6 Rejoiceth not in iniquity, but rejoiceth in the truth; Beareth all things, believeth all things,

hopeth all things, endureth all things. 8 Charity never faileth: but whether *there be* prophecies, they shall fail; whether *there be* tongues, they shall cease; whether *there be* knowledge, it shall vanish away. 1 Corinthians 13:4-8

We are living in the hour of the Spirit of Truth. I believe the Spirit of Truth is going to take the place of these other things. I believe God is bringing it strong into our lives that we may know the truth, that we may walk in the truth, and obey the truth, and He is giving us His peace which is beyond anything that we can understand. Our human love does not compare with God's love, we fail with it, we get affected by it, our emotions are involved with it and they get torn up. But if we allow God to remove these things from our lives so that His pure love is in there, His pure love will respond to every situation, so then we will not be affected by the situations. I grant you that many times it's very difficult for us to be silent when we feel we need to speak out. It's difficult for us not to be angry when situations arise that try us to the limit. God gets angry too, remember that; but His anger is different from human anger, His anger is different. Our anger has many things that His angry love does not have, the anger that comes out of us is not God-given, mostly. It's selfish, it's self-centered, it's self-seeking, it's all of these things, it's jealousies, it's vain glories, it's boastful, and it gets haughty. God's love does not do any of that, sometimes God will come in His anger, but He is saying to us that He wants His love to take the place of this human love that is not good. God is perfecting us with His love; but you know you don't learn this overnight. You learn it by processing, we learn it by the processing God is doing in our lives. I remember a time in my life when the Lord said to me, "You cannot love your husband, you cannot love your children more than you love the stranger coming out there." Well, that was a pretty big wallop.

How could I do that? I could do that only if I permitted Him to take from me that which is not like Him and not His love. We have love one for another but it may not be God's love, it may be just a thing we feel one toward another. But when we have God's love in us, then we feel differently. God does something that helps us in any situation we don't know how to handle. I can tell you in my life I have had many trying times. We have trying times with others, trying times with our children; and trying times with ourselves; because we kind of like our own lives. But with God's love in your life you try to be careful concerning what you say, what you do, and how you act.

Some of us do not exemplify God's love very much, do we? How many know that? You know that, and sometimes when we don't exemplify His love teachers get angry, schools get torn up, and bad spirits run everywhere. It's then we have to get in and pray and get rid of these. Well, God is perfecting you too with His love. And one day you'll be able to stand in a congregation of people, and you will only feel God's love for one another, because He will take everything else out of your life if you will let Him.

One thing about the Lord, sometimes we slip up and we say and do things, but just as soon as we do, something happens, how many know that? Pretty soon we're aware that really wasn't the Lord in us but it was our own reactions. God is perfecting us in His peace, He's perfecting us in His love.. He said all these things are going to pass away, but HIs love shall never pass away, His peace will never pass away, His joy will never pass away. God wants that, under any and all circumstances, we rest in His peace, we rest in His love, and we have His joy. In the midst of all kinds of circumstances, the Lord will keep us, He is saying here,

> And the peace of God, which passeth all understanding, shall keep your hearts and minds through Christ Jesus. Philippians 4:7

> Heaven and earth shall pass away, but my words will not pass away. Mat. 24:35, Mk. 13:31, Lk. 21:33

Not just your heart, but your mind; these things will not change. Heaven and earth will pass away, but Jesus said His word will *NEVER* pass away. And what He is doing in our lives is forever. Amen? He's removing from us the hindrances; He's removing from us things so that we're trained here to go out to other countries; it's very, very important that we are trained in the little things. It's very important that God's love is what is governing our lives. It's very important that His peace is there, and His joy is there because that love, peace and joy which He has imparted to us is going to tell the world out there that Jesus loves them. And this is why we need to allow the Lord to remove the junk out of our lives and let the flesh go, so that we can have His pure love abiding in us.

We do not exemplify God when we go in fits of anger. We do not exemplify Him when we want our own ways, doing our own things. God wants us to come into a relationship with Him, with His pure love, and peace, and joy so that we can flow together in whatever God has for us to do. With His peace, His love, and His joy I can tell you that I have much more patience and I have much more endurance at 80 years than I had at 40 years. I can tell you that He's done a lot in my life, and He can do the same in yours. It doesn't have to take 40 years to do it, all it takes is a determination to let the Lord change your life. And it can be done quickly, if we really choose to walk in His love, and let go of the human stuff we call love.

God'a love doesn't expect anything in return. We get hurt by our love and it hurts us. God's love doesn't hurt us, God's love doesn't expect anything in return. It's pure, it reaches out and loves everybody without wanting anything in return. If you want something in return, then there must be some of your own desires there and your own love. God is saying, "Don't expect anything from other people. Love them with the love of the Lord, and they will respond with God's love." But if we show anything else, we're hindering what God wants us to do and what He wants us to be. He wants His love to change our lives, but it's up to us. It's not conceited, it's not arrogant, and it's not inflated with pride. It's not rude, God's love does not insist on its own rights or its own ways for it is not self-seeking, it's not selfish, it's not touchy, it's not fretful and not resentful. It takes no account of the evil done to it.

We need that, don't we? We need that because pretty soon somebody does something to us and something rises up inside of us in defense. Many years ago, God was dealing with me, and I said, "But God, I don't deserve that kind of treatment." How many of you have ever said that? "God, I don't deserve that kind of treatment." I was pretty stubborn about it; because I was sure I was right. I was positive I was right, that I didn't deserve that kind of treatment. But God said to me, "You hard head! It doesn't matter whether you deserve it or you don't deserve it, let go of it!" This is what happens with us: we act a certain way, and the Lord says,

"Just let go of it, it doesn't matter." God's love doesn't take notice of those things, God will give it to you. There was one man that we had helped an awful lot, and he was a preacher. We had helped him and got him out of one situation and then another. We prayed him out of it with his family and with all kinds of things. And then he'd talk about me, he'd call me, "That woman, she, that woman," you know. All the years that I helped him, I said, "How long Lord am I going to have to help this man and not even get any respect out of him?" He didn't even remember my name, after years and years of helping him.

Well, sometimes these things we have to put up with, but how do we react to it? I just said, "Lord, I think I've helped him long enough." But the Lord didn't feel that way. I said, "But, Lord, I've had enough." One time I said, "Lord, I'm going to put the padlock on the door, and I'm not going to have any more people come ever again." I only said that a couple times to the Lord. But the Lord said, "Now you know you're not going to do that."

God's love is what has to reach out and change hearts, children's hearts, adult's hearts, just everybody's hearts. God's love has to do it. We can't do it by beating them, yelling at them, or screaming at them. We can't do it by getting angry with them. It does not work that way, sometimes we feel like it, and sometimes we do it, but it doesn't work.

God's love endures all things. There comes a time when God says, "That's enough." There have been a few people in my life that God has brought me to them and said, "You don't have any more to do with them, it's finished." Thank God, not too many, but because the Lord said it was enough, we drew back, and those people never went anywhere with God. They went backwards because God knew what was in their hearts. God knew the very things they were doing against Him, and against His Spirit, and His Word, and against His love.

Love endures long and is patient, the Lord wants to build up in every one of us this love that endures long and is patient. Most people and young people don't have any patience, but patience is something you learn by enduring. And sometimes I hear remarks one to another, and I can tell they're not enduring anything. They are not showing God's love, and they are not enduring anything. But God says His love endures, it's patient, it's kind. We need today to hear His Word and say, "Lord, fill me with Your love. Fill my heart, fill my mind, fill my body with Your love." It must be precept upon precept, precept upon precept and line upon line, and line upon line, here a little and there a little.

God will change your life but this is the hardest thing we have to do, why? He says, "I'm only putting My love in you so that when you go out to other countries they're going to know that you've been sent by Me, and that My love is in you, and they are going to respond to My love." Every human being, unless they've turned reprobate or let powers of Satan totally control them, is effected by God's love. God is calling us to intercede, to pray, to love one another, to uphold His Word, to show His love even when the situations are unlovely. God is so faithful to us that we need to be faithful to Him. We need to remember this Word that He's giving to us.

> Finally, brethren, whatsoever things *are* true, whatsoever things *are* honest, whatsoever things *are* just, whatsoever

things *are* pure, whatsoever things *are* lovely, whatsoever things *are* of good report; if *there be* any virtue, and if *there be* any praise, think on these things. 9 Those things, which ye have both learned, and received, and heard, and seen in me, do and the God of peace shall be with you. Phil. 4:8-9

Paul said, "...do:", he didn't say, "You heard me say it," did he? Now listen to it: "... and heard, and seen in me, do:". Isn't that is a little more than just hearing it? "and the God of peace shall be with you." God imparts with every Word that He gives out of the Bible, He imparts it to you. You have the right to receive it, you have the right to make it your very own, because He's giving it to you. So, if you want to come up a little higher in His love, receive it! He's giving it to you so that you can be like Him. He's giving it to you, because Paul said, "What you have learned and received and heard and seen in me..." Paul was the example that God used to show the people His love and His Word. Receive that which you have both learned and heard and seen in me," Paul said, "...do:" — "...do: and the God of peace shall be with you." He's imparting it to us even now.

Now, I declare unto you He's going to try you, I know so. So,

> And be ye kind one to another, tenderhearted, forgiving one another, even as God for Christ's sake hath forgiven you. Ephesians 4:32

Amen? Then love one another with the love of God, and it won't bounce back. We won't become sour, or bitter, or resentful, but it will flow from Him and from you to others.

When we went into Africa and into India God sent us. He had prepared us so that when we went we would not be afraid. He prepared us in His love that when we went they would know it was God. We went into cannibal villages, we went into all kinds of villages. We went into a Moslem village, and the man who loaned us his jeep was a Moslem. We went in there and the minister with us said, "Well, we won't be here long, because they're Moslems."

Do you know what happened? I said, "Lord, You give me the words that are going to touch the hearts of those people." And He did! And they gave their lives to Jesus, they came out of the fields, and they kept coming, and they kept coming. There was a man and a woman there, and the Lord told me to give them this Bible and said to tell them to nurture and train these people by the Spirit of the Lord. They stood there and tears run down their faces and they said, "We know that's God, because God has put it in our hearts to do that for the people." We had to go, we couldn't stay, we don't know what happened, but we do know God put the care of it with someone whom He had appointed to take care of them. Never once did they say to us, "It isn't God" or "It isn't God's love." They knew it was God's love. They knew that God had sent us. And this is true of our lives; we need to know what we have *heard and seen* by His love, then Paul says, "...do:"; do it.

The greatest of these is love. I thank the Lord for what He is doing in every one of our hearts, we need to press in. We need to allow His love to take the place of all the other things that we have that are not beneficial to us, or to Him, things that won't work. Only God's love is going to work, only His joy is going to work, only His faith operating in us. The greatest of these is His love.

God wants to bring us into that relationship so that we can do the right things when we're dealing with people and dealing with children so that we don't damage them so that His love prevails over everything else. I grant you there is an aggravation by the enemy, a lot of times, that we would like to do something different, but I believe God is bringing us into a place with Him that will help us to have understanding and patience with every situation.

God wants to put His love in us and remove the "mixture," so that He can make us strong to go out there and win people of any faith or all faiths to Him; because He's the One that's going to do it. We just need to let Him do it. Paul said here:

> Let your moderation be known unto all men. The Lord *is* at hand. Philippians 4:5

And if he felt He was at hand.

How much more do we know that He is at hand, and that we need God to prepare our hearts so that He can use us in touching other hearts and other lives?

Father, we thank you for the Word. We thank you Lord Jesus, that you made the way for your perfect love to be in us. God, we thank you that you so loved the world that you gave Jesus to us. And Jesus, you so loved us that you died for us. Now Lord, let us so love you so that your love will saturate our hearts, our minds, and our entire beings. Impart your love to us, Jesus. Let all these other things pass away but let your love remain in our hearts and in our minds. We thank you, Lord Jesus, for your Word, but we thank you for what you have done to bring it to pass that we might have this love abiding in us. That we might reach out to the unlovely, the uncared for and those who don't have anybody to love them or to care for them. God, teach us your ways that we may walk in them, and that we might fulfill your Word according to your Word, and according to your Spirit.

Jesus, we thank you for this Word, let it sink into our hearts, let us move by it. Jesus, let us desire more than anything to let your love fill every part of our being until others can see you, Jesus, in us. Lord, we thank you for this Word. Let it penetrate to the depths of our being, Lord, and cause us to respond with your love, that we might love one another. Bless your people, each and every one, let your love penetrate into them, and let these other things pass away. But let your love remain, Jesus, let your peace remain, let your joy remain, Lord, that our joy may be full.

We thank you for this Word. Jesus, we praise you now for the impartation by your Spirit, of your love, your peace, your joy, your righteousness, and your holiness. Lord, make us to be your people that desire you more than anything in this world, that you might use us to bring the world to you. Jesus, we thank you for this precious Word that you've imparted to us. We thank you for the growth by your Spirit, Lord, according to your Word. We give you glory now, Jesus, and we praise you for everything you have done and are now doing, and we thank you for the finished work of your great love. In your Name, Jesus, we ask for your love and for your glory. Amen.

PASS IT ON

I appreciate the word of the Lord. It says God left the responsibility to us to pray for the world for He commissioned us to take this gospel of the kingdom to the entire world, to all nations, that we might be a witness to them. I want to read something. The Lord brought this scripture to my mind,

> Ask of me, and I shall give thee the heathen for thine inheritance, and the uttermost parts of the earth for thy possession. Psalm 2:8

This is what God is saying to us. Jesus prayed for us that we would become one with the Father, the Son, and the Holy Ghost, and that we might become one with one another. The only way we can take this gospel to the entire world is to know that it is Christ in us that will do it, by His Spirit. It is only by His Spirit that it is accomplished. Jesus came to set the captives free; but He left the responsibility with us to bring this gospel of the kingdom to the entire world that we might be a witness to all nations. Then the end shall come. When I was very young the Lord gave me this scripture and I purposed in my heart to ask of Him.

> Ask of me, and I shall give thee the heathen for thine inheritance, and the uttermost parts of the earth for thy possession. Psalm 2:8

I believe because I asked, He has given me a burden and a vision. My heart is crying that this gospel of the kingdom of Jesus Christ shall be preached to the uttermost parts of the earth to the heathen, a burden that we will see this word which the Lord has spoken taken to all nations.

Do you know that if we do not ask God for the heathen that maybe no one will pray for them? The only way that anyone can come to Jesus Christ is for someone to pray for them. That is why it is important for us to pray specifically for certain people or things. God will answer! But if we have no one to pray for them they cannot come, because somebody has to ask God to save the heathen, and ask Him for the uttermost parts of the earth.

Every one of us should have that in our heart, that we are determined to be in that place that God has called us to be. We must be ready as God directs us to go in the entire world and all nations that this gospel shall be preached. It is our responsibility that God has given to us. We need to understand that, unless we pray and ask, God cannot give it. He has left with us a commission to go into the entire world and preach this gospel that Jesus died for on the cross. Our foundation is laid in Him, not in religion or denomination, but in Jesus; and in Him we live, and move, and have our being.

The Lord is holding us responsible to take this gospel of His love, His peace, His joy, righteousness, and holiness to the ends of the earth. The Lord has made it possible for us to flow together by His Spirit to accomplish what He wants done on the whole earth. This year is going to be a mighty year for God with great responsibilities because He is going to require more of us than He did last year. He is saying it is time to wake up, and arise, and let God use us the way he wants to, to use us to take this gospel to all the nations.

Soon the Lord is going to come. Soon the responsibility He has given to us, we will have to answer for. If we have been obedient He is faithful; and God wants us to be faithful in everything. Through the love He placed in us He wants us to flow together as one in the love of God. It is through this love that God will demonstrate Himself to the heathen out there. It is this love of God, manifested in us, that is going to cause the utter most parts of the earth to know Jesus.

I know the Lord is speaking to us that our responsibilities are going to be greater. He is awakening us to arise. The Lord is come; the glory of the Lord has risen upon us!

> Arise, shine; for thy light is come, and the glory of the LORD is risen upon thee. Isaiah 60:1

Rise and shine for thy light is come! He has come in us that we might go as His witnesses to the world; that through the glory which Jesus has in us the world might know him. We need to arise, we need to shake ourselves, we need to allow that responsibility that God has for us to come to us. We need to be faithful!

God has called us, and Jesus made it possible for us to obey Him, and He will bring it to pass. Let our hearts be stirred by the word tonight. As we arise to make ourselves ready in the word of God, by the Spirit of the Lord He will do it. It's through Jesus Christ and Him alone, for only He can do it, may God bless you.

May you realize that in this New Year that He has given us a new day and a new year in which to obey Him? With great rejoicing and thanksgiving may we know the joy of serving our God and walking with Him? We need to rejoice because the Lord reigns in all the earth! He does care what happens to the heathen and what happens to the utter most parts of the earth. We need to arise with hope for He is the hope of glory, God bless you this year, I will give it to you! When the Lord gave me this verse I knew it was from the Lord. Do you want to hear it? I will give it to you,

> Wherefore he saith, Awake thou that sleepest, and arise from the dead, and Christ shall give thee light. Ephesians 5:14

I tell you God gave us a certain scripture and I believe we will see this scripture fulfilled just as I saw the last year's scripture fulfilled. Last year it was,

> For with stammering lips and another tongue will he speak to this people. To whom he said, 12 This is the rest *wherewith* ye may cause the weary to rest; and this *is* the refreshing: yet they would not hear. Isaiah 28:11-12

He said that those people would not hear it, but that we will hear it and we are going to see it come to pass.

> This is the rest wherewith ye may cause the weary to rest and this is the refreshing. ... Isaiah 28:12

He said this people will hear it. I saw the total fulfillment of it this year; I saw God do great and mighty things. Through the miracle of the wheat alone I saw this scripture come to pass.

How did God use the wheat? It caused the weary to rest and this is the refreshing. I believe God is going use to do something mighty as we shake ourselves from our sleep. As we come out of that which has been like death it will allow us to move. We are going to see God move in the resurrected lives in us, awake thou that sleepeth.

I want you to remember Isaiah 60:1,

> Arise, shine; for thy light is come, and the glory of the LORD is risen upon thee. Isaiah 60:1

The Lord shall move by the power of the Holy Ghost down to man. The other part blessed my soul so much. When I was in the Philippines God burned the other part of it into my heart.

> ... and from the islands of the sea. Isaiah 11:11

shall be converted unto thee. Arise; shine for thy light is come! He said, "Wake up! The multitudes of the sea shall be converted unto thee."

I tell you when I got to the Philippines God said, "This is the people I have told you about." In America we are so complacent, our churches are so dead. One thing I noticed in the Philippines was that when they worshiped, when they sang to the Lord, and gave Him glory, that I said to God, "This is the people you have been looking for; this is the people I have been looking for." The Lord said, "You have found them. They have given glory unto My name and they worship Me with all their heart." I said, "God, I thank you." I felt right at home with them for they gave God glory. When I came home I heard things about America. I said, "Lord, I thank you for the Philippines, because you are going to rise up a people that are going to the ends of the earth, and they will not be stopped." I thank God that every barrier is going to come down; and I told them to rise up your light is come and the glory of the Lord has risen upon you. Prepare yourself to obey God and He will use you.

The resources of that country are virtually untouched; whereas our resources are taken away from us. But God will raise up a people over there that will do what He wants them to do: to feed the hungry, to help the poor, and to do the things that God commands us to do. I believe that God has turned from America because we have sold out to the Communists. The food that belongs to the rest of the world has gone to the Communists and we're letting the rest of the world starve. Because of the facts that are before us: they plan to starve two and one half billion people as fast as they can starve them. It's not only in America but in every other country in the world. Someone must rise up and obey God so He can feed the hungry and take care of the poor. The 1990 statistics are that three hundred and fifteen million dollars in grain was given to Russia from the USA; when only twenty million went to meet the needs of the rest of the world and in America.

Do you think God is going to smile on it? What is happening to us? Drought and freezing! Our crops are frozen and the end result is famine. And when famine comes to a nation, when we forget God, when we refuse to acknowledge him, He will send the famines and pestilence. God has to have a people to obey him! God told me to pray for America. We've let the enemy destroy our schools, and we've let them bring abortion to destroy lives. The truth of what is happening is to destroy the human race: to starve them to death by their acts of turning from God. He will put judgment on the nations that do this.

God is saying we had better wake up and be obedient to Him. Satan plans to rule this earth in ten years. We better wake up and realize the seriousness of this word. Take heed to what the Lord has spoken. Famine will come to the nation that forgets God. Pestilence will come to that nation that forgets God; but woe to them that try to destroy the church. God has a plan, for the glory of the Lord has risen. Glory to God! We praise you God! I thank you for this word, let us arise, and let us go forth, and do what You would have us to do.

We give you glory, Lord Jesus, that we would run to the ends of the earth. We give you glory and we thank you for each one. Preserve us blameless before you. In Jesus name! Amen.

"The life of the Lord is upon your life."

God wants to extend the years of your life because of those that have been disobedient to thy heavenly call. Caleb was not able to die because the promise had not been fulfilled of entering the promised land. God has made you a promise.

Young men and young women must come forth to take this into a far greater dimension to reach the unreachables and touch the untouchables.

God is extending the years of your life, touching your body, strengthening your bones, your eternal being.

For this decade YOU MUST LIVE to see the turn of the century, to see the generation that are now at your feet raised up to be a generation of giant-takers.

God says, "I am going to give you the privilege.

I am strengthening your bones, your heart, your arteries, your veins, that you may live in health in these next seven years."

And there's more, but God says so that you may see the turn and even the returning...

So, Lord, I bless her now and I thank You for the power of Your Spirit that is upon this life today, in the name of Jesus, and I thank You for doing it.

Amen. Hallelujah!

Prophecy through Kim Clement
to Rev. Agnes I. Numer
September 23, 1993

Kút- Poki
Soboba Lighthouse
Mishkan
Where He Dwells

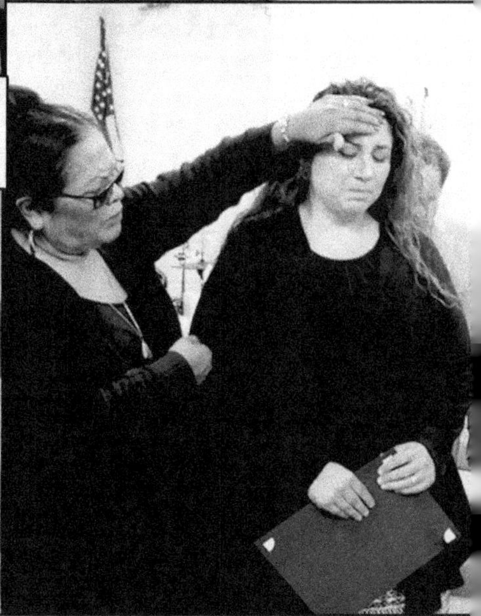

Soboba Training Center

Facing Page: Pastors Virginia and Albert Duenaz Kut-Poki Church - Soboba Indian Reservation, CA

Pastor Karen and Leon Vielle - Eagle Plume Ministries - Blackfeet Reservation Browning, MT

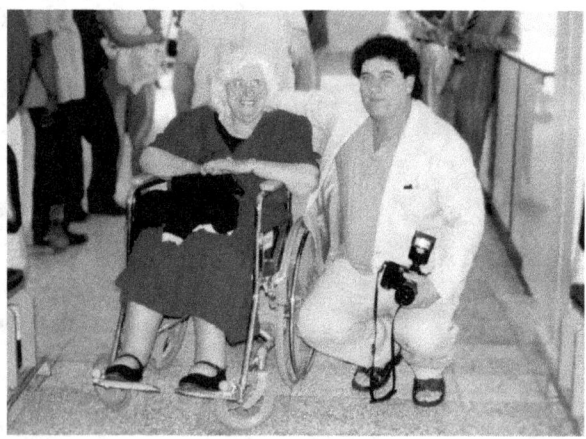

Agnes I. Numer with Cliff Feldman in the Dominican Republic

ABOUT THE AUTHOR

God uses ordinary people in extraordinary ways. Agnes Irene Numer is one of these.

"One day in 1954, I was washing dishes," "All at once I felt this 'mighty presence.' God told me to read Isaiah 58."

And so began the call....

Born August 5, 1915, in Racine, Ohio. Passed away July 17, 2010, in Lancaster, Calif. She grew up in Belaire, Ohio, and has lived in the Antelope Valley for 56 years. She was known by many as the Mother Teresa of America, Rev. Agnes I. Numer gave food to the hungry, clothes to those that had none, and love to the unloved. She trained many to walk in the footsteps of sharing Gods love to the nations.

Agnes I. Numer, one of 9 children, was born in Racine, Ohio. When she was only 11 years old, her God-fearing mother died. At 16 years of age, God miraculously changed her life and placed in her heart a burden for the nations of the world.

A few years later, Agnes attended Eastern Nazarene College in Massachusetts. As she stood in front of the mission board watching her colleagues receive their commissions to go abroad, God told her that she would not go in her younger years but in her later years. Forty years later, almost to the day, Agnes I. Numer stood on African soil for the first time. Since then, she traveled all over the world, bringing the Gospel of the Kingdom to the nations.

In 1954, God revealed to Agnes, in minute detail, Isaiah 58 – His plan for the nations of the world. Always had a heart to help those in need, God began sending people to her door. Local markets and farmers began to contribute food. An international organization reaching out to help a world in need was born from this small beginning.

In 1979, God spoke to Agnes to start a missionary training center where people could be trained by the Spirit of the Lord to meet the spiritual and natural needs of others. God began sending people from all over the world to her 10-acre ranch in the Antelope Valley, CA.

According to the plan that God had given her, she established training centers where leaders received a vision, a hope, a plan and the principles of God's Kingdom. Those leaders continue to passionately put these principles into practice around the globe. And the vision continues.

- facebook.com/AllNationsIs58
- twitter.com/AllNationsIs58
- instagram.com/AllNationsIs58
- amazon.com/Agnes-I-Numer/e/B089T8MBZZ?ref_=dbs_p_ebk_r00_abau_000000

More Sermons by Agnes I. Numer

Volume 1

A Call to The Nations
A Full Surrender
Allow Him to Abide
A New Heart
A Righteous People
A Short Time Yet
A Strange People
Beatitudes
Becoming Naturally Spiritual
Be Confident: God Will Finish What He Has Begun
Behold I Do a New Thing
Beyond Christmas
Blessed Is the Man the Lord Chooses
Bought With a Price
Bringing Forth a Flow

Volume 2

Brotherly Kindness Complete in His Love
Brotherly Kindness, Demonstration of God's Love
Brotherly Kindness – Equipping Word
Brotherly Ministry – The Natural and The Spiritual Working together
But to Praise Him!
By His Power
By His Power The Christian Way

By My Spirit
Call to Fast
Change Us
Come And See the Works of God
Coming Out into a Wealthy Place
Come to The Mountain
Dying to Ourselves
Faith
For One Purpose
God Is Showing Himself
God's Calling

Volume 3

God's Love & Glory
God's Love
God's Love Must Be Perfected
God's Purpose
He That Hath Ears
His Protection by Our Obedience
How Precious Is Our God
Imparting His Glory
Jesus The Vine
Let God's Love Come into Us
Let Him Be King
Let Us Hear
Meet The Needs of The Poor
Miracle In Our Minds
My Word Shall Remain
New Birth and Foundation

Volume 4

Nothing Can Separate Us from The Love of God
Open His Commandments
Perfected In His Love
Prepare Our Hearts
Preparation to Go to The Nations
Prophets, Priests, And Kings
Psalm 24
Putting On the Lord Jesus Christ
Spiritual Warfare
Stephen
Taking Responsibility
That The World May Know
The Armor of Intercession
The Call from Macedonia
The Carpenter's Son
Entrance into The Kingdom

Volume 5

The Fine Water That Perfects God's Love
The Fruit of The Vine
The God of Battle
The Lord Thy God in The Midst of Thee
The Lord Will Joy Over Thee
The Mountain Shall Become a Plain
The Only Way
The Pride of Life
The Scope of Sommer Haven
The Spirit of Truth Has Come
The Way God Provides
The Willing and Obedient
The Word Is Nigh unto Thee

The Wrath and Mercy of God
There Is Power in The Name of Jesus
They Shall Be Ashes Under the Soles of Your Feet
This Record of His Son

Volume 6

Thy Word Is a Lamp
Isaiah 58 - Time to Run
Transfiguration
Under New Management
Waiting Upon the Lord
We All Have a Choice
What Does He Require of Us?
The Vision No Longer Tarries
Allowing God's Perfect Peace
The Plumbline
Lord, You Have Ordained Peace for Us
Faith Worketh By Love
Come Up Higher in His Love
Pass It On

Volume 7

The Making of a Man of God
Become Strong Soldiers of the Cross
Revelation of Jesus Christ – Ezekiel 1
The Making of a Man of God - Ezekiel 2
I Have Made Thee a Watchman – Ezekiel 3
Training by the Holy Spirit
Being a Servant — 1 John 3
The Character of Jesus Christ in Us

Of No Reputation
Be Guided by the Lord
Die to Self, Live for Christ
A Willing Sacrifice

And More...

Get these books and more at: seldomseenpress.com

Or in a bookstore near you or online at:

Amazon, Barnes and Nobel, Apple Books and more...

Hear Rev. Agnes I. Numer at Mixcloud:

https://www.mixcloud.com/revagnesarchives/

See Rev. Agnes I. Numer on YouTube

www.ingramcontent.com/pod-product-compliance
Lightning Source LLC
Chambersburg PA
CBHW071441070526
44578CB00001B/187